FIFTY YEARS
HONORING OUR PAST, LIGHTING THE FUTURE

The Story of Southwestern Oregon Community College
By William A. Lansing

SOUTHWESTERN
Oregon Community College

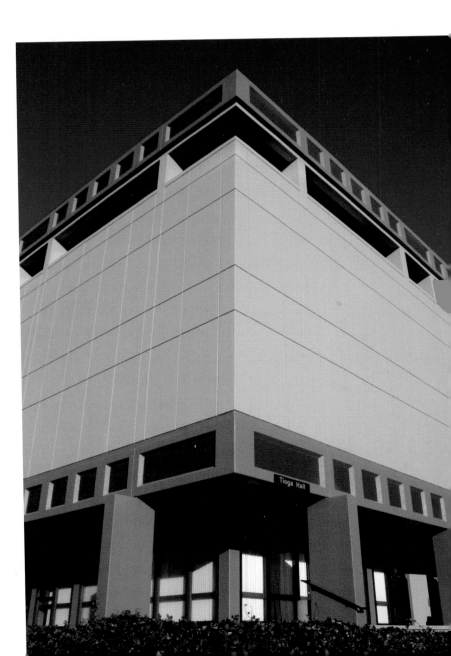

Permission may be sought directly from
Southwestern Oregon Community College
1988 Newmark Avenue, Coos Bay, Oregon 97420

Library of Congress Control Number: 2011934911
ISBN: 978-0-615-51546-5

Printed in the United States of America
10 9 8 7 6 5 4 3 2 1

Book design by Anne Farrell-Matthews
All modern photos on cover, introductory pages and pages 14, 38, 39, 78, 91,
120, 124, 132, 133, 141, 144, 156, 158, 162, 184 by Anne Farrell-Matthews.
Photo of basketball players courtesy of www.coosbay-northbend-oregon.org

*Back of dust jacket (clockwise): Presidents Jack Brookins and Wendell Van Loan
examine the swampland that will become Southwestern Oregon Community College;
Tioga Hall, courtesy of The World newspaper by Lou Sennick; Graduation, 1964;
Graduation, 2011; Forest trail floating bridge building crew, 1973; Nursing students in
simulation exercises, 2009.*

A beautiful campus rose from swamp-land . . . and transformed into a modern community college.

TABLE OF CONTENTS

APPENDIX 167

FOREWORD

Southwestern Oregon Community College holds an important place in the community college movement in Oregon; it was the first community college chartered after the law changed in 1959 that allowed college districts to be created. It was the people of the South Coast who led the charge to get the law changed. It was the people then and it continues to be the people today that support and keep the College alive.

When I became President of Southwestern Oregon Community College in 2008, my first goal was to deal with a serious financial crisis facing the College. State funding dropped from 46% to 29% of our current funding, and local property taxes dedicated to supporting the College were limited by ballot measures passed in the 1990s. As the country began to struggle with the "Great Recession," enrollments continued to increase at the College along with the demand for excellent service. Our institution, like other public colleges across the nation, was being held in an economic vice. I also knew I needed to complete the building of a satellite campus for SWOCC in Curry County that was started by President Steve Kridelbaugh and the Board of Education several years ago.

Concurrent with the reality of managing the daily business at the College, I realized that the 50th anniversary of the institution was quickly approaching – May 1, 2011. This was an important event, not only for me and the students – past and present – it was also important that the community realize what the College had meant for them and vice-versa. We needed something to commemorate this milestone. We needed to locate our first graduates from 1962, find the 50 student body presidents, recognize 50 years of nursing student graduates (the longest ongoing degree program), and organize our history for others to enjoy for years to come.

As SWOCC turns 50, the College still enjoys the support of the community and people of the South Coast, one of whom is Bill Lansing. Bill is a longtime trustee of the SWOCC Foundation, a retired CEO and author of several books. I was aware of Bill's previous books on local history and decided to ask him if he would help write the history of the College. He asked what I wanted in the book and I told him I wanted something special; a book that students, professors and the community at-large would cherish in their libraries, was interesting to read, was first class, and documented important events in the 50-year history of the College. This book not only documents the history of SWOCC but also reminds the reader about other important events that occurred during the last five decades, both locally and nationally. I am very pleased to present this book on the 50th anniversary of Southwestern Oregon Community College as written by Bill Lansing.

Dr. Patty M. Scott
President
SWOCC, 2011

PS – I am interested in hearing about your favorite SWOCC story! Please send stories or feedback to us at www.socc.edu/50th.

PROLOGUE

For those old enough to remember the end of World War II and the educational demands that the returning GIs placed on the existing universities, few may recall the important role that President Harry S. Truman, who never graduated from college, played in establishing the community college system in America. In 1947, President Truman, with the support of the congressionally authorized GI Bill behind him, established the National Commission on Higher Education for American Democracy. It was their assignment to find a solution to the challenge posed by the returning veterans along with developing concurrent programs for minorities, women and working adults. President Truman was clear in his beliefs:

> *"A democratic community cannot tolerate a society based upon education for the well-to-do alone. If college opportunities are restricted to those in the higher income brackets, the way is open to the creation and perpetuation of a class society which has no place in the American way of life."*

One of the conclusions reached by the Commission was a need to expand the two-year college system across the country. In fact, the name "community college" came from the Commission's report as it was applied to the institutions designed to serve a local community's higher education needs. The community college system was therefore restructured to provide three core tenets: (1) to provide alternative avenues for the first two years of a four-year university education; (2) to provide occupational training and issue two-year degrees; and (3) to provide developmental education and counseling for adult education.

President Dwight Eisenhower continued the push started by Truman.

> *"Communities or groups of neighboring communities will do well to consider new two-year community colleges. Experience in a number of areas has demonstrated that with carefully planned facilities and programs, community colleges can be highly effective in affording readily available opportunities for excellent education beyond high school."*

Bob Bower, a retired English professor at SWOCC, expressed his feelings succinctly in a recent interview for this book:

> *"I was very idealistic when I graduated with my master's degree and believed that those who spoke about how best to transition high school graduates (or high school dropouts) to a four-year degree program or eventually to the world of work were really missing the story. I thought that the community college education was the real key to bridging those students to the four-year colleges or into the communities for vocational work."*

Bower was dead on correct!

As these two-year colleges began spreading across the American landscape, several terms were used interchangeably to describe them. Terms such as community college, junior college, technical college, and technical institute were frequently used interchangeably to describe colleges such as Southwestern Oregon Community College. For example, Harvey Crim, a local accountant with Georgia Pacific Corporation in Coquille, was asked one day back in the mid 1960s if he ever considered working for a community college. Crim's response was "What's a community college? I drove over to Coos Bay and spoke with Dr. Van Loan, the President of the College, who I recognized immediately as one of my instructors at Oregon State University. He offered me the job of business manager. I accepted and stayed at the College for 26 years." Apparently Dr. Van Loan's pitch about the community college intrigued Crim!

To help alleviate any further confusion, the following terms will be used in this book:

Community colleges are comprehensive institutions of learning that provide: (a) a general education preparing students to transfer to a four-year college or university, (b) career and vocational education, and (c) adult and continuing education programs.

Junior colleges are institutions whose primary mission is to provide a general two-year education leading to transfer and completion of the baccalaureate degree at a four-year college or university. Junior colleges often provide continuing education programs as well.

Technical colleges and technical institutes refer only to those institutions awarding no higher than a two-year degree or diploma in a vocational, technical, or career field. Technical colleges often offer degrees in applied sciences and in adult and continuing education. Also, there are technical institutes with curricula that extend to the baccalaureate, master's, and doctorate (e.g., Massachusetts Institute of Technology, Rensselaer Polytechnic Institute), but these are not community colleges.

That is not to say that small two-year colleges or universities of higher learning did not exist in America before the Truman era. During the colonial times, for instance, a charter from the King of England was required before a college could be "authorized." However, many small communities throughout New England created colleges in the absence of such a charter. These had rather finite curricula and in general tended to be religion-based institutions with small enrollment of the elite.

The first real effort to form a "junior college" in America was recorded in 1893 when Reverend J. M. Carroll, President of Baylor University, proposed that smaller colleges with a reduced curriculum would be cheaper to operate than a full fledged four-year university. The smaller schools would provide the first two years of college study and allow "graduates" from these small Baptist colleges to transfer to Baylor for the final two years of education. Undoubtedly his thoughts were fueled by the flood of immigrants coming to the United States around the end of the 19th century. His thesis was pragmatic, rooted in the reality of the high cost of financing multiple four-year universities across Texas and Louisiana. From this action, the first official truly American two-year junior college was born.

As the nation's universities spread out across the country in the early part of the 20th century, national associations were founded to align themselves around the roles of the community college, the junior college, the research university, and the liberal arts college. The Association of American Universities (AAU), founded in 1900, advanced the agenda of the research institutions. The Association of American Colleges (AAC), founded in 1914, defended the role of the small four-year colleges and advanced the cause of liberal learning as the primary aim for higher education. The American Association of Junior Colleges (AAJC), begun in 1921, provided a forum for the two-year institutions (including high schools that provided two-year collegiate programs), women's colleges, military institutes, private junior colleges, and technical institutes. In 1907, for instance, the California Legislature passed an Act permitting high schools to offer the thirteenth and fourteenth grade level of education on their campuses.

The Oregon Community College Association (OCCA) was not established until 1962. Southwestern Oregon Community College was a charter member along with Treasure Valley, Central Oregon and Blue Mountain colleges. [1] In the beginning the OCCA was divided into two segments – administration and faculty – each with their own agendas. In the early '70s a new division was added to accommodate the needs and interests of students. This gave the student government organizations on campus a voice at the State level.

In 1984, Dr. Dale Parnell, Oregon's Superintendent of Schools from 1968 to 1974, wrote a book called "The Neglected Majority" in which he described a whole group of students that were not likely to earn a baccalaureate degree. According to Dr. Parnell, "the 2000 census indicates that 26% of the adult population in the United States held a baccalaureate degree or higher. That meant 74% did not." [19]

After serving as Oregon's Superintendent of Schools under Governor Tom McCall and serving a stint as President of Lane Community College, Parnell moved to Washington, DC as President of the American Association of Community Colleges – a position he held until 1991. His first lobbying effort was to stop the Reagan administration from eliminating the Department of Education and the Secretary of Education. According to Dr. Parnell, "they were trying to cut back on the role of the federal government in education of any kind as well as cutting the funding for vocational education in particular" - a major tenet of the community college. The opposite point of view stems from the belief that education is the responsibility or purview of each state and not that of the federal government. That debate continues today.

Fifty years ago there were over 600 community colleges in America. Thanks to people like Dale Parnell, today there are well over 1,200 community colleges in our nation touching the lives of 12 million students who take advantage of the programs they offer – pre-university and vocational/technical courses. [2]

Before we tell the 50-year story of SWOCC, let's pause a moment to take a closer look at some of the Oregon politics surrounding the establishment of its community college system.

In the 1920s, the Oregon Legislature established 13 junior college districts in the State. The legislation required the approval of the registered voters within each district before it could be officially created. The bill failed for lack of structure and funding. It would take Oregon another 40 years to get serious about developing a comprehensive community college strategy.

In 1941, the Oregon Legislature provided a way to organize post-high school job training institutions in the State. However, no funding accompanied this bill either, and it led to rather meager results. In 1949, the Legislature allowed local school districts to create extension centers for the purpose of offering college-level courses. These programs were generally held in the evenings at local high schools, but no official campus or taxing district was formed. The State was still not focused on Dr. Parnell's "Neglected Majority."

In 1947, the Oregon Legislature provided a special appropriation to fund the creation of what was known then as the Oregon Technical School on 822 acres at an old Marine military facility in Klamath Falls, Oregon. Some 800 students enrolled when the doors opened in July of that year. It became known as Oregon Institute of Technology (OIT) in 1957, but no other two-year college would emerge under the Act.

In 1951, the Oregon Legislature created the State Board of Education to oversee K-12 education as well as the State's community colleges. House Bill 143, known as the Junior College Plan for Oregon, required that any two-year college district formed must be part of the public education system in the State. However, no college districts were formed under this original Act until certain amendments were added six years later. The major amendment that was added allowed college districts to form districts that were independent of the State Board of Higher Education, but would still be part of the general public education system of Oregon. Programs were started in Bend and Klamath Falls that were extension centers of learning under the University of Oregon. Instructors would teach two nights in Bend then drive to Klamath Falls and teach classes for two nights.

Shortly thereafter, the Bend School District Board of Education called for a special election to form a community college district under the State Department of Education System for their region. The vote was positive, but no other college district would form until further legislation was passed allowing community college districts to form with independent boards of directors elected from candidates from within the district to set operating policies for the college. It was into this political environment that Henry Hansen, a longshoreman from Coos Bay, stepped up and launched his effort for a local community college in southwestern Oregon.

In 1959, Oregon Senate Bill 260 was introduced that again provided for the creation of 13 independent community college districts within the State. These college districts could be formed outside the System of Higher Education, each with its own elected board of directors. These college districts would offer comprehensive community college programs that included vocational education and lower division transfer courses, as well as other adult education programs for people who were no longer subject to the compulsory school law. Counseling and guidance services would also be part of the community college program. Again the results were dismal due to the lack of State funding to support the legislation, but at least Oregon was developing a system of community colleges. [3]

Peter Sorensen (current Lane County Commissioner and a former SWOCC graduate) explained how his father got involved as a French/German language and photographic instructor on the SWOC (sic) campus in 1962:

> *"One of the reasons my father, as well as others on campus at the time, got involved in the community college movement was the fact that they really believed in the fundamental tenets of the institution. The whole notion of a comprehensive post-secondary institution where businessmen, lawyers, plumbers, carpenters and other journeymen could provide practical and relevant education to students was very appealing. Instructors did not have to have an education certificate granted by the State which was a prerequisite to teach in an Oregon public school – implying that people with 30 or 40 years of on the job training in a technical field or simply as life experiences just might have something of value to impart to eager young students wanting to follow a similar career."*

In1961, the Oregon Legislature got serious about creating a viable system of community colleges throughout the State, and with the passage of Senate Bill 440, 13 college districts were finally funded. This time the Legislature set aside $851,822 for community college operations and $850,000 for capital construction as the districts began to form. A formula for reimbursement was established at the State level whereby each college that qualified for one full-time equivalent student would receive $433 for operational expenses (FTE refers to a student carrying 36 credit hours of college transfer courses - later changed to 45 credit hours or 510 clock hours per year). Capital construction reimbursement was set at $1,500 per FTE student.

In 1991, Oregon's Legislature, in order to raise the standards for education throughout the State, passed the Oregon Educational Act for the 21st Century. That Act set the State on a course of educational reform in K-12. The law was strengthened and clarified by the Legislature in 1995 and called for rigorous educational standards to evaluate student performance and their progress. The effort was supposed to improve the competency of high school graduates who wanted to continue their education at college. [41]

The law was controversial and introduced the Certificate of Initial Mastery (CIM) – an examination to be given to sophomores in high school to measure progress against a State standard – and the Certificate of Advanced Mastery (CAM) to be given to high school seniors. Tests were also administered to specific grade levels in the elementary schools. As the reader will soon see, there was a serious decline in the abilities of high school graduates to master the entry level of college courses in English and mathematics. It is not the purpose of this book to critique the results of this legislation, except to state that SWOCC would find itself teaching more of the remedial courses to freshmen enrolling at the College. While Southwestern Oregon Community College was adapting to changes it saw in the students, it was also coping with profound changes in the communities it served.

Community College Funding in Oregon

As the reader works through the history of Southwestern Oregon Community College as told on the following pages, it is important to have an understanding of the evolution of the financing of the community college system in Oregon. Local control and governance of community colleges has undergone little change over the last fifty years, but the control of community college funding mechanisms changed dramatically. From their inception in the early '60s until 1989, the operational funding of the Oregon community colleges primarily came from local property taxes – which gave a close connection with the community it served.

During the 1990s, Oregon voters passed three different tax initiatives that had a dramatic impact on the funding of all public schools in the State: Measures 5, 47, and 50. Taken together, these tax limitation measures fundamentally changed the relationship between community colleges and the district citizens by limiting local property tax revenues available to community colleges as well as K-12 school districts. The State now distributes the majority share of community college operational funding as provided through the State's general fund budgeting process. Currently, SWOCC receives about 30% of its revenue stream from the State. [42]

Today there are 17 community colleges operating on 60 campus centers spread across Oregon. The State Board of Education provides oversight for the colleges and appoints the Commissioner of the Department of Community Colleges and Workforce Development (CCWD). However, it is very important to remember that each individual community college is governed by a locally elected board and led by the President they appoint.

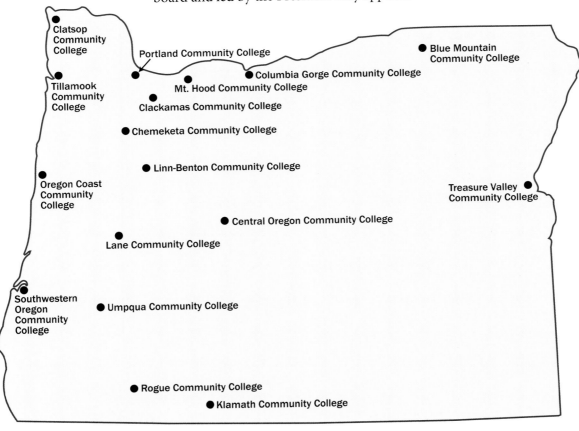

Community Colleges of Oregon – 2010

In 2007 alone, over 90,000 students enrolled in these two-year institutions throughout Oregon. Over the past 50 years, SWOCC has had a remarkable story to tell about its history – from early classes being provided in renovated buildings in several locations throughout Coos County, to classes being offered at the campuses on Empire Lakes, the Curry Campus in Brookings, the Gold Beach Center, and the Port Orford Center - all providing opportunities for students.

The following is SWOCC's story. It's about how the College maneuvered through the adversities of funding, national trends and local economies to provide wide and diversified opportunities to the people of the region. While there are many ways to break apart its 50 year history, this book is divided by decades. One could have just as easily redefined the epochs as follows:

1957-1961 – The Visionary Years
1961-1964 – The Formative Years
1964-1985 – The Building Years
1985-1990 – The Fine Tuning Years
1990-2005 – The Building Years - II
2005-2011 – Redefining the College

THE VISIONARY YEARS

Henry Hansen - 1908 to 1996. Several years after the College district was formed, Hansen was recognized by the Oregon Community College Association by receiving the Howard Cherry Award for his work in forming the district. The award is named for a former Portland legislator who was deeply involved in education.

Stubborn Tenacity and Grit

Fifty years ago, the thought of a community college in southwestern Oregon was but a dream in the minds of a few industrious local people. One in particular was a retired longshoreman by the name of Henry F. Hansen who worked tirelessly to make this dream a reality. Union leaders in general wanted an opportunity for their children to gain access to a college education, but the main universities in Oregon were quite some distance away from the Coos Bay region. In fact, there were no post-secondary campuses on the Oregon coast.

Hansen made numerous trips to Salem - with the financial support of his local International Longshore and Warehouse Union (ILWU) - to cajole the State Board of Education and the Legislative Subcommittee on Education that the people of southwestern Oregon needed and deserved a school of higher learning in order to better prepare young people for the future. Union members explained that when they could, they would put five dollars in a "kitty" to help offset Hansen's travel expenses and reimburse his time away from work. By the time the petition drive was underway, the Oregon Legislature passed a new law that required a petitioner to put up a one thousand dollar bond that would be forfeited if the public election following any petition drive failed. The ILWU put up the bond. The isolation from the mainstream of Oregon's institutions of higher learning made access to post high school education by the citizens of the Coos County region all but impossible. The Legislature agreed and sent Hansen back to map out a college district for the region.

Ralph Stuller, a former board member at the College and vice chairman of the State Board of Education in Salem, had this to say about Henry Hansen:

> "Henry Hansen was the most stubborn, one-track man. This (campaign for a community college in Coos County) was almost like a holy crusade to him. He did not accept any argument against forming the College. Anyway, this is Henry; although sometimes you get tired of having him bend your ear, he'd get on the phone and talk to you for an hour and an half at any time at night. You couldn't get away."

Another of the original SWOCC Board members went on to describe Hansen this way:

> "He was a rugged individualist, in some respect he kind of reminded me of old Don Quixote when he said to Sancho Panza let's make another run at the windmill. Henry had real courage in his convictions and visions...I think we all admired him because after all he was the one that really motivated the whole program; he had a certain way of getting through barriers."

At first, Henry had a rather grandiose concept of a college district, one that ran from Lincoln County in the north to the California state line in the south, then eastward to Ashland, Medford and Roseburg. A public hearing was held at the Coos County Courthouse on that proposal and all the representatives from east of the coast range arrived to insure that no such district would include them. In fact, of the 63 people present at the hearing, all but three were opposed to the large college district. So the first district boundary was reduced in size and authorized by the State Board of Education in 1960 as follows:

> This matter coming on regularly for hearing before the State Board of Education in Salem, Oregon on the 4th day of August 1960, all members of the State Board of Education being present except May Darling; and due notice of said hearing having been published in the counties of Coos, Douglas, Lane, Curry and Josephine, being the territory described in the petition for the formation of the said Area Education District in the manner described in ORS 341.730; and the Board having considered all testimony and evidence

presented at the hearing and having considered the territory which may be benefited by inclusion with the proposed Area Education District, the Board finds that the following described territory should be and shall constitute the territory and boundaries of the said Area Education District and that any other territory described in said petition could not be benefited by the formation of said Area Education District;

NOW THEREFORE, based on the testimony and evidence introduced at said hearing, and the said findings,

IT IS HEREBY ORDERED that the boundaries of the Southwestern Oregon Area Education District shall constitute and include the following described territory; to wit:

(See ballot measure on page 7 for description.)

As a side note, the first efforts to form the College district were temporarily thwarted by a group of voters from a portion of the district who overturned the first signature petition in court. In his own words, Hansen described his feelings about that action in an interview in 1979:

> *"But there was this little group, gave their mailing address as Port Orford, and they went into court and got an injunction against us to stop the effort. Well, I didn't have any money to go into court and I wasn't going to do it. One of the charges was that the title of the petition was insufficient; that it was misleading.*
>
> *"Well, everybody that signed (5,000 citizens of the area signed the petition to form the district) knew what they were signing. I didn't have the money to fight it in the courts, and it was a waste of time anyway, so I'd just go back to the next legislature and amend the law. So I was debating whether to go ahead on it or not and what to do. You know, everybody thought I was nuts.*
>
> *"The next legislature was a Republican legislature, and Mark Hatfield was Governor. I concentrated on the education committee – good people, reasonable, but real frugal. We finally got a law put together, a lot of patches and what not, and we got that law passed, and I hurried up and got a couple thousand more signatures and we had ourselves a community college district; the first one in Oregon and the beginning of the whole system."* [8]

With new realities in place and revised legislation backing a college district that stretched along a rather narrow coastal strip from Florence to Port Orford, on May 1, 1961, Hansen went to the voters who approved a new taxing district to support a new two-year college. At the same time, a new board of directors was elected that included Henry F. Hansen (chair), Leslie King, Orville R. Adams, G. E. Albertson, and Wilfred A. Jordon. In June 1961, the State Board of Education approved Southwestern Oregon College (sic) as meeting the requirements of Chapter 602 of the Oregon Laws concerning education centers and community colleges and SWOC (sic) could open for business.

Mrs. Melvin Floyd (left) and Mrs. Jesse J. Laird (right) spent four hot days at the Coos County Fair in 1958 collecting signatures on the petition to form the College district. Members of the local unions fanned out throughout the district in order to get more signatures on the petition until they got the requisite amount.

Henry Hansen (far right) at an ILWU picnic in 1958 with the community college sign showing the original large district boundaries.

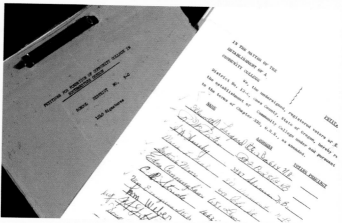

The original petition to form the College district.

Reflecting on the work that went into gaining the signatures necessary to place the proposal on the ballot, Jesse Laird, a local labor leader, said: "The College started in a tent." What Mr. Laird was referring to was the fact that his wife and Mrs. Melvin Floyd secured voter signatures on a petition while sweltering in a tent at the Coos County Fair grounds in August 1958. According to Laird (who may have taken a certain amount of liberty with his contribution to the College):

Jesse Laird ca 1990
Reflecting on his earlier days,
Laird said that he completed
the eighth grade with one-half
year at Marshfield High School,
before quitting school in 1926 to
go to work in the woods.

"Me and other members of the local International Woodworkers of America (IWA) Union along with cooperation of the members of the local International Longshore and Warehouse Union (ILWU) fine-combed the highways and byways of southwestern Oregon for additional signatures. My territory was from Coaledo south to the California line. You see, the original district ran from Florence to the California line east to Roseburg. We had to get 10% of the registered voters to sign the petition. That was fairly easy to do. As I recall, we got about 5,500 signatures. There was some sort of error in the title of the petition, so Henry Hansen got that changed and we needed only 500 more signatures to get it on the ballot. I was working for the Coos Bay Lumber Company at the time and they gave me the time off, because they thought it was a good project and supported out efforts." [4] [57]

The voters approved the district boundary of the College, which ran from Florence in the north to Port Orford on the south. The Florence area withdrew from the district following a regional election in that part of the district on March 15, 1962 and the Port Orford School District 2J was officially removed from the College district by the SWOC (sic) Board of Education on April 26th of that same year. The comments made at the hearings focused on the distance students would have to travel from either town to reach the Coos Bay/North Bend campus. Even though Hansen made it plainly clear that students that had to travel from outside a 30-mile radius from the Coos Bay/North Bend area would receive a five cent per mile reimbursement payment, both ways, the areas wanted out of the College district.

Hansen pushed hard to get the students from these outlying areas to campus in order to increase enrollment. But in the end, neither the SWOC (sic) Board of Directors nor Dr. Van Loan, its new president, resisted the move to shrink the district as the voters on the margins of the district were in reality too far away from the campus to benefit. Since the College Board had to get approval for the operating budget each year, the College did not want a large segment of the voters on each end of the district to continually oppose the College. In the end, it left the taxpayers of western Douglas County and all of Coos County to fund the College district operations - that is until 1995, when Curry County voters agreed to join the College district.

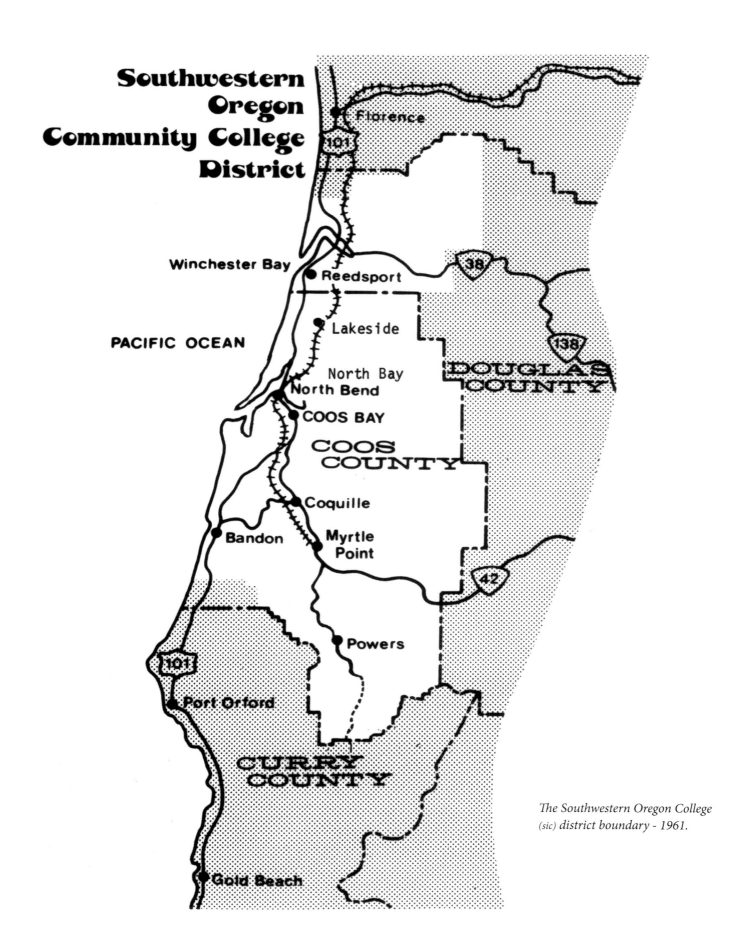

Southwestern Oregon Community College District

Florence

101

Winchester Bay

Reedsport

38

PACIFIC OCEAN

Lakeside

138

North Bay

North Bend

DOUGLAS COUNTY

COOS BAY

COOS COUNTY

Coquille

Myrtle Point

Bandon

42

Powers

101

Port Orford

CURRY COUNTY

Gold Beach

The Southwestern Oregon College (sic) district boundary - 1961.

IN THE MATTER OF THE
ESTABLISHMENT OF THE
SOUTHWESTERN OREGON
AREA EDUCATION DISTRICT

BEFORE THE OREGON STATE
BOARD OF EDUCATION

BALLOT
Election May 1, 1961

Vote YES or NO. Mark X in the square for the Answer Voted For

Shall an area education district community college to be known as the Southwestern Oregon Area Education District be formed and established pursuant to the provisions of Chapter 341 ORS which shall constitute and include the following described area:

All of Coos County, all the territory comprising Coos Curry County School District 2J, Port Orford Langlois, Douglas County School District No. 9, Gardner school District No. 105, Reedsport, together with the unorganized territory (not in a school district) between the southern part of School District No. 105 and the Coos Douglas County line, the Lane Douglas County Joint School District No. 97J, Florence all as presently defined and recorded in the proceedings of the respective District Boundary Boards of the several counties in the State of Oregon above described.

Following the acceptance of the vote of the people within the College district and after a year of operation at the College, the State Board of Education established the two main objectives of the College:

The following definitions are given to provide a common basis for discussion of the present and proposed programs at the college: [66]

General Education *is defined as courses that serve as a part of a two-year general education terminal curriculum or complement vocational-technical occupational preparatory curriculums, and that are designed to assist the student to function effectively as a member of a family, a member of a working group and a citizen of his community, state, nation and world.*

Vocational-Technical Education *is defined as education designed to develop skills, abilities, understandings, attitudes, work habits and appreciations, encompassing knowledge and information needed by workers to enter and progress in employment on a useful and productive basis. It is an integral part of the individual's total education program and contributes toward the development of good citizenship by developing physical, social, civic, cultural and economic competencies."*

The first official organizational meeting of the new College Board of Education was held on May 18, 1961 to iron out a budget in order to ask the district voters to approve an operating levy. At this point, Hansen had his college district, but no money with which to operate it. He and the Board were determined to open the College that fall. The Board put Maurice Romig temporarily in charge of the daily details. He would end up being the one, along with approval of the Board members, who assembled most of the original faculty – many of whom were already teaching college courses scattered in high schools around the Coos Bay area. Romig was also the one that recommended to the Board that two scholarships be given to students attending classes at the College from each high school within the district. In terms of a later popular movie, the Board surely operated under the presumption that "if we build it, they will come."

In July 1961, Hansen went back to the voters and requested an operating tax base of $362,649 to run the College for one year. This was in addition to the $375,000 of State and federal money, $51,625 in tuition, and $66,885 of reserves. The total budget for operating the College in that first year was $856,159. The district voted 3,365 in favor and 2,021 against. Interestingly, this percentage of approval was a greater margin of victory than when the votes were tallied a few months earlier to form the district itself. The actual vote for the levy - by the 26 voting districts - was as follows: [18]

But where would the SWOC (sic) college campus(es) be located? There were no funds to construct a campus and how much money would it take to run it? And as they say, "the Devil is in the details," but Hansen and the new board were up to the task. Another possible reason that might have underpinned Henry's success at the polls lay in his continual promise that the College district would never bond itself for construction costs. Time would reveal the inaccuracy of his promise. [20]

District	No	Yes
Arago	15	29
Bandon	157	92
Bridge	9	46
Broadbent	14	17
Charleston	48	69
Coos Bay	314	624
Coquille	148	640
Dora	4	26
Eastside	36	151
Empire	48	206
Fairview	5	28
Florence	241	22
Gardiner	3	35
Gaylord	7	8
Glasgow	26	112
Lakeside	42	93
Langlois	155	4
McKinley	6	16
Myrtle Point	81	250
North Bend	200	592
Port Orford	337	27
Powers	17	48
Reedsport	34	82
Riverton	17	33
Sitkum	1	24
Sunny Hill	49	91
TOTAL	2,012	3,365

Total voters eligible to vote in the election – 27,850 – only 19% cast their ballot!

One of the first jobs of the Board was to determine the salary they would offer professors, administrators and the college president. After considerable debate, the salary to be offered to full-time faculty members with a master's degree would be $7,500 per year and $14,000 per year for the college president. A search was conducted that summer for a new president and 15 applied for the job. Dr. Wendell Van Loan was chosen as the first president of the College. He was a professor of education at Oregon State University in Corvallis. He was not officially appointed the president of the new college until August of that year. When Van Loan took charge, Romig stepped aside and became the dean of vocational education at the College. (See Appendix for the biographies of the College's presidents).

From a strategic point of view, Van Loan seemed vehemently opposed to federal aid to public education. According to Professor Croft, the first history teacher at the College, had Van Loan been receptive to federal aid, the SWOCC campus could have been built in one fell swoop. Unlike Bend, which used federal funds to quickly bring its campus on line, it took SWOCC many years to fund and grow its campus.

Dr. Wendell Van Loan, president of Southwestern Oregon Community College 1961-1964.

As Professor Bob Croft, who was one of the original faculty, remarked:

"We were able to open on time. We had a basic curriculum – a little history, a little science, a little English, a little psychology. We filled in the gaps with part-time instructors as needed. There was a real espirit d' corps. You were always one jump behind yourself all along the line. It was tremendously exciting and adventurous." (52)

Further describing Van Loan, director Wilfred Jordon recalled:

"Wendell was one of those types of people that gave everybody a chance to participate. He was a great one for writing little notes. He had this little stubby pencil, gosh darn I often thought I was going to send him a big pencil; he would pull that little old pencil out to make a note. We had several dinner parties at his home."

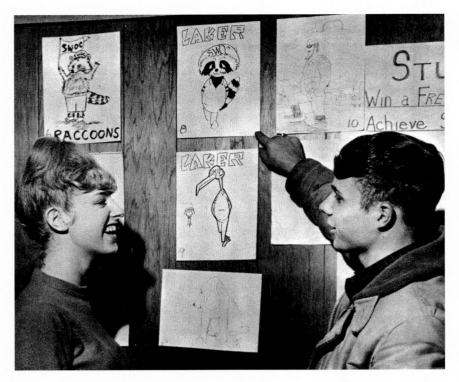

The final selection of the school mascot.

Local relatives of the College mascot can often be seen at night patrolling the campus grounds.

All colleges need a name, team colors, logo and a mascot around which the student body and community can rally, and the new two-year college in southwestern Oregon was no different. But the new college name went through several iterations. The transformation started in February 1962 when James Ross, a student at the College, suggested "Southwestern Oregon College" for the official name of the College and "Lakers" for the athletic teams. Another student, Steve Thorwald, suggested the school colors be navy blue, red, and white, and a third student, Dennis Dawson, requested the mascot be a scrappy "raccoon." All of these recommendations were accepted by the school's Board. For their creative suggestions, Mr. Ross received a $6 gift certificate for naming the College and another $5 certificate for the team name - both redeemable at The Hub store in downtown Coos Bay. Mr. Thorwald received $4 for selecting the school colors.

The current SWOCC logo used today.

The SWOCC athletic logo.

The SWOCC Mascot, Rocky.

The evolution of the College logo – a lighthouse – is a bit more obscure; no one seems to recall how it was selected. However, according to Carol Vernon, a retired art instructor at the College, the original lighthouse logo was a bit ornate, something one might see on a dollar bill. President Bob Barber asked Ms. Vernon to redesign the logo, but leaving the lighthouse as the central theme. Asked to describe the rationale behind the logo, Ms. Vernon went on to say that it was symbolic of a solid landmark to give students confidence that there was something stable lighting the way for their future.

Further proof that Southwestern Oregon College (sic) was indeed a functioning campus was publication of a college newspaper – *The Southwester*. The first copy of *The Southwester* newspaper was published on Friday, November 10, 1961.

The original name of the College, Southwestern Oregon College (SOC), drew protests from Southern Oregon College (SOC) in Ashland as the acronyms were identical. In April 1962, Southwestern's Board of Education changed the official name of the College to South Western Oregon College or SWOC. However, the students and faculty did not particularly like separating the words South and Western or even how some pronounced the new acronym. According to Sheldon Meyer, former vice president of Administrative Services, locals understood the meaning, but to an outsider pronouncing SWOC it "sounded like you were clearing your throat!" In 1965, as the result of a specific legislative requirement, the word "Community" was inserted into the name. Henceforth, the College became known as Southwestern Oregon Community College – or SWOCC - that is until recent times as discussed later!

The first campus newspapers came out every couple of weeks. The aim of The Southwester, as reported in the first edition, was to present campus news without prejudice and provide a free-speech outlet for all sides of an issue, all while adhering to journalistic standards. At first, the newspaper was printed by the Empire-Charleston Builder and most recently, The World Newspaper. However, due to budget constraints the print editions have been discontinued. Today The Southwester's online publication is updated with articles and features weekly.

The original sign at the Airport campus.

Today, the College's name seems to be undergoing potentially new iterations. President Dr. Steve Kridelbaugh hired a marketing consultant to see if the name carried any influence on recruiting or gift giving. Again the jury was split - some on campus prefer the old name while others wanted to call it SOCC; yet others wanted the campus to be known simply as Southwestern. In an interview with the current college president, Dr. Patty Scott, she said, "The community can call us whatever. We just want them to call."

The west entrance sign was made out of Redwood and was designed by Hal Buckner - a SWOCC student who went on to become a world famous artist.

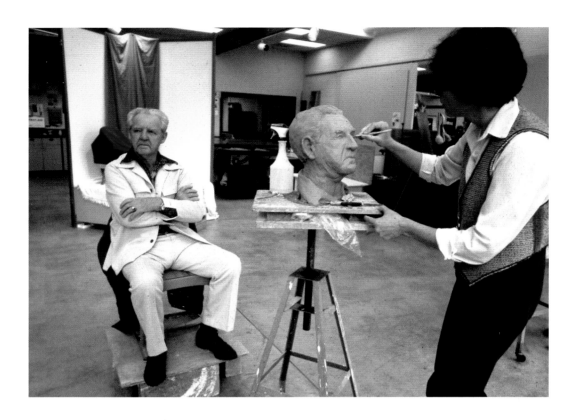

The statue of Henry Hansen welcomes all to the SWOCC campus and rightfully holds the title of "Father of the College." The bust was created by Carol Vernon during an art class she taught on campus. The project for every student was to sculpt a bust of Hansen. Apparently Henry sat as the model for the class over a five-week period. According to Vernon, "As he sat for hours as our model, we heard lots of Henry's stories as a longshoreman."

HENRY HANSEN
LONGSHOREMAN

WORKING MEN & WOMEN THROUGHOUT OREGON'S
SOUTH COAST FOLLOWED HENRY AND HIS DREAM
OF A COMMUNITY COLLEGE FOR THE CHILDREN OF
ORGANIZED LABOR. PETITIONS WERE CIRCULATED
—AND SIGNED. HIS ENERGY AND THE EFFORT OF
ORGANIZED LABOR LED TO THE CREATION OF
SOUTHWESTERN OREGON COMMUNITY COLLEGE
—THE FIRST COMMUNITY COLLEGE IN OREGON
OPERATED UNDER A STATEWIDE SYSTEM.

SOUTHWESTERN OREGON COMMUNITY COLLEGE
WAS ESTABLISHED BY THE VOTE OF THE PEOPLE
ON MAY 1, 1961.

THE FORMATIVE YEARS

The next obstacle faced by the new College Board was to find places where the teachers and students could come together in classrooms. In 1961, School District 9 offered to lease the East Branch Building of Marshfield High School to the College for vocational and technical programs. A couple of classrooms at Sunset Middle School of School District 13 located near the North Bend Airport were also made available to the College. The Sunset school was built during World War II to accommodate the children of the military personnel serving at the North Bend Airport. A lease was signed to use the old Navy gymnasium near the North Bend Airport along with another small building that would be used for classrooms in the same complex. The original administration for the College was in the same building where the classrooms were located. But shortly after opening the College, the administration, faculty offices and library were moved up on the hill above the Airport campus in order to make more room for classrooms.

Administration

Sunset Middle School

Gymnasium

The original SWOC (sic) campus was located at the North Bend Airport – 1961.

The recent history of the Airport dates back to World War II as follows: On February 3, 1943, the Department of the Navy signed a Letter of Agreement with the City of North Bend for use of 617.9 acres of the municipal airport, improvements thereon, and abutting tidelands as a Naval Auxiliary Air Station. The Station was commissioned on May 10, 1943 as the U.S. Naval Auxiliary Air Station, North Bend, Oregon, an activity of the U.S. Naval Air Center, Seattle, Washington. At various times during the history of this facility several squadrons comprised of many different aircraft - torpedo bombers, dive bombers, transports, fighters and observation planes - were stationed at North Bend. The primary mission of the Station was stated to be the administration, operation, maintenance and training of Fleet Units. Additional missions were to serve as a base for inshore patrol, to provide aviation facilities for a naval and army squadron, and to provide landing facilities for lighter than air patrol craft (blimps). The installation was utilized primarily as a training base for Navy pilots and aircrews from 1943 to 1945.[83]

The main College administration building used in the early 1960s was built in 1943 as a naval officers' barracks. After the War, the property was sold to the City of North Bend and for a period of ten years it was leased to private parties and used for a hotel – and as some of the old timers recalled - a hotel for brief stays! The hotel ventures were unsuccessful and the City repossessed it in 1957. The building sat idle until SWOC (sic) leased it from the City in 1962. It would serve as College administrative and faculty offices along with the bookstore. Since the building had sat empty for several years and vandals had damaged the windows and exterior, the College had considerable expense in bringing it up to a standard where it could be occupied.

The doors to the "campus" were opened in the fall of 1961 and 815 students (or 256 FTE) registered to attend. As we investigate the decades ahead, the reader will begin to appreciate the importance of the Full Time Equivalent (FTE) concept to campus life. The tuition was set at $65 per term. In those early years, students that had to commute a significant distance were given a "travel allowance," and those living more than 50 miles from campus had their tuition waived. There were 15 full-time faculty members and 11 part-time instructors ready to go as the doors opened. The students were mostly young men and women of blue collar families, proud to finally have a college nearby. There was a true sense of pioneer excitement and adventure. The students were there to learn and help mold the character of the campus. Admission to the College was defined in the first catalog as follows:

The College accepts students of good moral character who provide evidence of suitable preparation for work at college level. The law provides that a student may enroll at the College if he (or she) is: (1) a high school graduate, or (2) a mature person, at least 18 years of age, who is prepared to undertake college work as evidenced by satisfactory completion of educational equivalency tests, or (3) is, in the judgment of the administrator of the College, capable of profiting from the instruction offered.

In an oral history tape on file at the SWOCC library, Dr. Van Loan described his memories of getting the College started back in 1961:

"My office at SWOCC was a potato bin. Our first classrooms and offices were in the old naval base on the sand spits of North Bend. We were the only campus in America that had a beer warehouse right in the middle of the campus. We were very grateful to the people of Empire who gave us the property to get started. As for the actual construction of the buildings, it was easy. When you start with bare ground and there isn't anything in your way, it is easy to do. You could lay out your roads, develop a plan for the campus and there was no difficulty at all."

To that his wife Lillian, who taught psychology at SWOCC, interjected:

"I don't think it was exactly easy. It was hard, hard work and often we were too tired to eat at night. There were decisions to be made every day and they weren't easy decisions." [54]

The original SWOCC campus parking lot at the North Bend Airport.

As Ms. Helen W. Ferguson, the first teacher of business courses at the new college, remarked in an interview back in 1978, "We had a seven-mile square campus because we were borrowing or leasing buildings (all over the county)." [43] Course offerings were split into two divisions – Liberal Arts and Science and Vocational training. Once the campus moved to its central location on Empire Lakes, the two divisions were further subdivided into Arts and Letters, Mathematics and Science, Business, Social Science, and Metals/Materials along with technical and special programs. [11]

As Professor Bob Croft remarked in a 1978 interview, "We really started from scratch. Everything was minimal, to say the least. We had minimal library facilities, but the students were terrific. We all tried very hard to schedule their courses so that they did not have to move from campus to campus very often during the day…"

Don Moffitt, the first business professor at the College, confirmed what others on the staff had said: "…we had no school, no buildings, no students, no teachers, no nothing, but we proceeded as though we could do it…" [64]

Professor Ron Lilienthal expanded on the topic by stating "many of us were hired two or three weeks before the start of classes and we had books to order, there were no course outlines, there were no textbooks, there was no library, there were no lab facilities---there was nothing. There were some war surplus desks that we refinished and moved in." [58] [60]

The original vocational classes at the College were generally taught in the evenings at Marshfield High School in Coos Bay. The high school shop facilities were adequate for the needs of the College. As mentioned earlier, vocational classes had been taught before SWOC (sic) was formed as they were available throughout the County for years. In fact, many of the vocational course instructors, as well as those who taught the more traditional classes of math and English, moved over from teaching evening classes under the Basic Education Program to being on the faculty at the College.

Karl Gehlert, a Board member at SWOCC from 1962 to 1971, expressed it best when he reflected back on the vocational and transfer course teaching at SWOCC at his retirement in 1971:

> "Before the day of the community college, the co-existence of these two programs (vocational/technical and liberal arts transfer courses) on a single campus was unheard of. There seemed to be an idea that there was some basic incompatibility between a student who wanted to weld and a student who wanted to teach. It is to the eternal credit of community college people that this notion is being shattered. To insure the recognition that there is dignity and value in any man's or woman's chosen field of work, students at SWOCC are encouraged to cross lines and seek instruction in both programs. And to insure that there are no real boundaries of barriers between the programs, faculty members at SWOCC frequently and commonly teach courses in both programs.

"Achieving this balance has been neither easy nor cheap, nor is the battle completely won. For too many years, peer pressure, pride and social acceptance have all been on the side of having 'going to college' mean nothing but embarking on a vocational goal that could be reached only via a four-year college or university." (55)

In the fall of 1962, a student lounge was "created" in the SWOC (sic) administration building on the hill above the Airport, where students from all the campuses were invited to relax between classes in bamboo Chinese-hat style chairs as they visited with friends, completed last minute assignments, or savored a light snack. Three picnic tables with benches were purchased to accommodate eating and studying.

The original SWOC (sic) campus building at the North Bend Airport housed the Liberal Arts and Science classes. Ron Lilienthal, the first biology and chemistry instructor at the Airport campus, said that all of his science classes were conducted in one building. The students did not have to travel to various classrooms scattered throughout Coos Bay to attend his courses.

To add to the relaxing atmosphere of the student lounge, a juke box was rented and new 45-rpm records were exchanged every month. All the money collected from the juke box was added to the Student Council treasury. Dr. Van Loan also donated several chairs, a piano, and a radio for use by students in the lounge.

Once the campus was started at Empire Lakes, a new student lounge was created that gave an opportunity for students and faculty to meet for general group discussions. Many faculty members had expressed the desire to spend time with students, just sitting in the lounge drinking coffee and talking over contemporary subjects. The goal was to break the barrier that normally exists between the faculty, as authoritative figures, and the students where their only contact was either in the classroom or the professor's office. At one point, these informal discussions were organized with a "topic of the week" posted ahead of time. Professor Bob Croft was usually in the middle of the discussions which often turned into political dialogues that might last a couple of hours – sometimes ending on a rather heated note!

Student lounge at the North Bend Airport campus. Copied from page 1, volume 1, number 1 of The Southwester newspaper – 1961.

In January 1962, the first slate of student government officers was elected and an effort was started to create the first emblem/logo for the College:

President –   Bill Gordon

Vice President –   Bill Cottell

Business division representative –   Terry McCracken

Collegiate division representative –   Dave Engle

Secretary –   Kristin Jorgensen

Technical/Vocational division representative –   Rockne Luckman

Treasurer –   Carol McCulloch

The suggested original designs for SWOC's (sic) logo were put before the faculty and students for a vote in 1961. As it turned out, neither design is used today, except for the lighthouse which became a beacon for the College.

In the beginning, intercollegiate sports were limited to those activities that could be done in the old Navy gymnasium during the day or in the evenings at local high schools when they were not in use. These included basketball and wrestling.

Row 1: J. Gaunt, J. Weekly, L. Gallaway, J. Gassman, B. Glazier, J. Doty. Row 2: R. Luckman, S. Merchant, M. Payne, B. Cottell, L. Dornath, S. Thorwald.

The *first* SWOC Basketball Team

Coach Bill Holmes

The first basketball team at SWOC (sic) in 1961. They had a record of 5 wins and 13 losses.

Outdoor sports were also limited as the "campus" did not have an official field. One of the sports that has endured over the decades at SWOCC is golf. Golf was a physical education option at the College in 1962. While the conditions were less than ideal, the class instructed would-be professionals how to chip out of the "rough!"

Golf class – 1962.

Bandon Dunes Golf Resort

Who knows, but it is possible that one day a grandchild of one of the college students seen above may get the chance to play on one of the courses at the world famous Bandon Dunes Resort just 25 miles south of the SWOCC campus.

Today, Bandon Dunes Golf Resort provides financial support for the College golf team and tournaments, and the College provides a caddy training program for those interested in working at the Resort. The relationship between the College and the Resort has been and will continue to be a great partnership.

As for social activities on campus during those early years, they tended to replicate those that were occurring in the local high schools at the time. There was a Harvest Ball in October, the traditional Christmas Ball where students returning home from attending Oregon State University or the University of Oregon could mingle with their friends who were attending SWOC (sic), the Sweetheart Ball, and the Homecoming dance. Once the veterans began returning from Vietnam in the late 1960s, many of these events were cancelled in exchange for providing more financial aid to the students in the form of scholarships. Today there are no formal dances held on campus. Informal social gatherings occur in the housing units or are organized by the Associated Student Government.

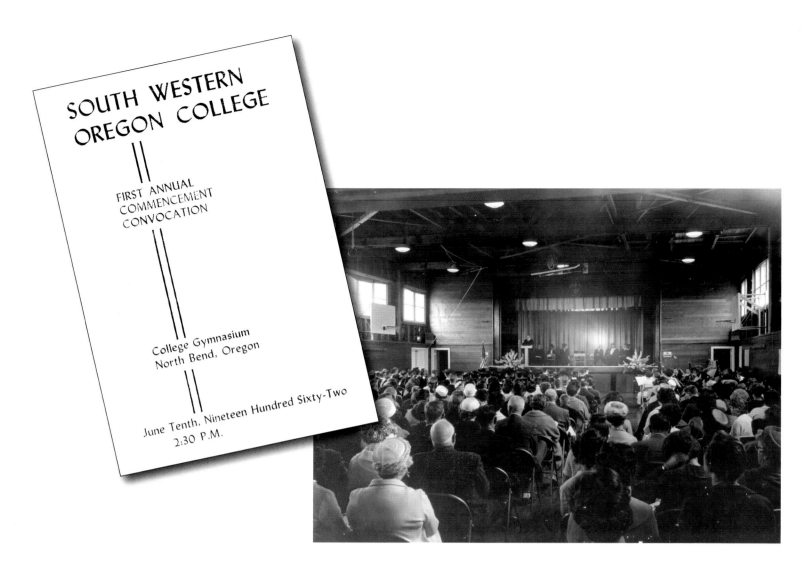

SOUTH WESTERN OREGON COLLEGE

FIRST ANNUAL COMMENCEMENT CONVOCATION

College Gymnasium
North Bend, Oregon

June Tenth, Nineteen Hundred Sixty-Two
2:30 P.M.

The first class to graduate from SWOCC in 1962 had 29 proud students. The actual graduation ceremony took place in the old Navy gymnasium at the North Bend Airport. One of the major drawbacks in using the old gym was its location next to the Airport where planes were coming and going. Due to the size of the gym, a loud speaker system was necessary and the frequency of the system picked up some of the radio transmissions between local pilots and the ground controller. As can be imagined, just when important announcements were being made or the keynote speakers were in the middle of their presentation, communication jargon could be heard over the loud speakers between the pilots and ground personnel. (The minutes of the SWOC (sic) Board of Education on July 8, 1963 stated that the City of North Bend had requested a lease increase for the gymnasium from $1 per year to $50 per month; the following month the Board passed a resolution increasing the lease of the gym to $75 per month for a period of three years.)

Professor Bob Croft, in discussing the preparation for the graduation ceremony with his colleagues, remarked:

> "If we were ever going to impress the community that the College was real and it was professional, we need(ed) to reach out to the community and provide 'Pomp and Circumstance' wherever possible. Doing a first class job at graduation with caps and gowns was a beginning."

The first graduating class included:

Associate in Arts – Marjorie Simmons

Associate in Science, Electronic Technology – Robert L. Brock, Irwin Roscoe Doty, James Lawrence Fitchett, Rehl M. Gamble, Fred Lee Harris, David Lloyd Kelly, Ronald Gene Lewis, Burl Estal Parrish and Lyle Leonard Psick

Automotive Technology Certificate – Gabriel A. Cabral, Roger J. Duvall, Karl Allen Long, Jack Otto Smith, Ronald L. Williams and Raymond Henderson, Jr.

Stenographic Certificate – Karen Elizabeth Anderson, Virginia June Caldera, Margaret F. Crumpacker, Inge Drennan, Bernice Anna Haliski, Margaret W. Kelley, Janet Marie Nielsen, Judith Kay Norton, Barbara Marvene Page, Penelope Lee Ray and Judith Rae Smith

General Office Certificate – Darrell James Bradley, Lucille M. Goheen and Frederick Sorensen

On the occasion of the 30th anniversary of that first graduation ceremony, *The World* newspaper carried an article commemorating the history of SWOCC and that first graduation commencement. The paper mentioned Marjorie Simmons as the first person to receive an Associate in Arts Degree from the College. Simmons enrolled at SWOC (sic) when the College opened in 1961 after taking several college outreach courses offered in the local high schools by some of the four-year colleges. Here is a part of her story:

"It wasn't easy. We had four children to take care of. My husband worked at Weyerhaeuser while I worked at various jobs around the area. I would take courses that would apply toward a degree, if I could get a babysitter. I attended classes all over. It was fun. Everything was makeshift and make-do. After SWOCC, I went on to Southern Oregon College in Ashland where I got my bachelor and master degrees. I returned home to North Bend and got a job teaching English in the North Bend High School until I retired 24 years after graduating from SWOCC."

South Western Oregon College

The Southwestern Oregon Area Education District Board of Education by virtue of the authority vested in it by law and with the approval of the Oregon State Board of Education has conferred on

Fred Lee Harris

the degree of

Associate in Science
Electronic Technology

with all the rights and privileges appertaining thereto.

In testimony whereof we have subscribed our names and affixed the seal of the College.

June tenth, nineteen hundred and sixty-two at North Bend, Oregon

W. L. Van Loan
PRESIDENT OF THE COLLEGE

Henry F. Hansen
CHAIRMAN, BOARD OF EDUCATION

1962 Associate in Science diploma from South Western Oregon College to Fred Harris.

The "original" Michigan Avenue
School before it burned down
in about 1972. According to
local history, the principal was
George Tate at the time and
the fire was started in the boy's
bathroom and all the children
were evacuated safely. The
school was rebuilt and burned a
second time. It was again rebuilt
and is currently known as the
Sunset Middle School.

The first annual for SWOCC
was called the EBB Tide.
According to Bernell Meacham,
"...the next couple of yearbooks
were called the Lacustrian. It
was a more formal presentation
of student and faculty portraits
and activities. The name was
chosen by the editor of the book
who said Lacustrian meant
'Lake Dweller' in Latin. The
yearbook sales were a disaster
and the only way the Associated
Student Government would
bail us out financially was if
we promised we would not
produce another yearbook. The
Lacustrian was short lived having only been published two suc-
cessive years – 1964 and 65." [61]

As the need for additional classroom space grew, in 1962 the College leased a
wing at the Michigan Avenue School in Empire where its business and technical
programs were housed. Roger Spaugh, the electronics instructor at the College,
recalled that his class was being held in the basement of the Michigan Avenue
School in 1962 when the Columbus Day storm came roaring through the area and
blew the door of his class room completely off its hinges. It would not be until the
fall of 1967 that education at the College would be offered at one location – the
new campus at Empire Lakes. [5] [58]

With growth came the inevitable friction between "management and labor."
In an interview in 1978, Professor Croft commented on this very issue from his
perspective as a faculty member at the College from 1961 to 1978:

> "We tried for some years to get the College faculty and administration to
> work in an environment where we saw each other as peers, friends and col-
> leagues, and we almost succeeded. Once the collective bargaining act went
> through, and the faculty went down that route, then the adversarial rela-
> tionship developed, regardless of your personal feelings. I think we would be
> much better off without the structure today." (See Appendix for Constitution
> of the Faculty Senate.)

From a structure perspective and after years of false starts, the Oregon State Legislature passed the Public Employee Collective Bargaining Act in the fall of 1973 that allowed both the faculty and classified employees at public schools to negotiate salaries, related economic issues, and grievance procedures. The employees at the College voted as to which union they wanted to be affiliated: The American Federation of Teachers, the American Association of University Professors, or the National Education Association.

Not all members of the faculty believed that a union was appropriate at the college level. Pete Sorensen relayed a story told to him by his father – a faculty member:

> *"Some of the faculty members at the time believed that a union was for people who worked with their hands in a mill, not for university professors. To convince the SWOCC instructors otherwise, the union brought in none other than Leonard Bernstein of the New York Philharmonic who was a member of the musicians union. They also brought Albert Schanker who was president of the American Federation of Teachers. They were brought in to schmooze the faculty and convince them to join the AFT."*

The majority voted for the American Federation of Teachers. A bargaining unit was formed and Kirk Jones was elected the first president. With the formation of the union, the College relationship was divided into three elements: The Faculty Senate that dealt with academic issues, the administration that dealt with overall management and worked directly with the elected Board of Education, and the union that dealt with salaries and working conditions at the College.

After almost 10 months of grueling negotiations between the SWOCC Board of Education and the SWOCC Federation of Teachers, an agreement was finally reached. Signing the contract was College Board of Education chair Lloyd Kuni and Kirk Jones, college librarian and president of the local American Federation of Teachers. Looking on were President Jack Brookins and the teachers' negotiating chairman Nathan Douthit.

Looking back on those formative years of the campus, it appears that President Dr. Van Loan followed the general rules set down by the Truman plan and that of the Oregon Legislature. The College not only provided lower division university courses, it also met the needs of the local older adult population by providing vocational training and short courses for working people wanting to improve their skills. It appeared from several articles in local newspapers and Board minutes that he gave no favoritism to any program.

One of the earliest vocational programs on campus involved training Practical Nurses - or PNs, as they were called - that evolved into an LPN program some years later. The program was started in 1962 by Mrs. Isabelle LaFond, a local registered nurse. Classes were held in a specially equipped classroom at the Michigan Avenue School. The facilities were small, so the class size was limited to 12 – 14 students. [12] Nurse LaFond retired after graduating her 13th class of practical nurses in August 1975. With the demand for nurses on an ever rising trajectory, SWOCC has continued to build upon the program started back then. Today there are 48 students enrolled in the nursing program – 24 first year students and 24 in the second year.

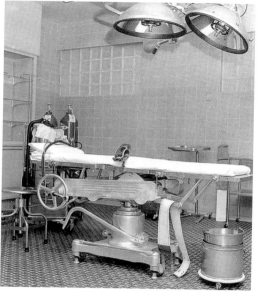

The operating room at Keiser Hospital in North Bend - 1958.

Nurse LaFond would always tell her students:

> *"The role of a PN is to provide nursing care to patients in those instances where the nursing needs do not require the constant attention of a registered nurse."* [7]

Both the Keiser Hospital in North Bend and the McCauley Hospital in Coos Bay cooperated with the PN program at the College. The original nursing program was a 48-week course with the first eight weeks devoted to classroom study followed by 40 weeks dedicated to actual hands-on hospital work. Those two hospitals are long gone, but the current nursing program works cooperatively with the local Bay Area Hospital as well as smaller hospitals throughout the College district.

Ralph Stuller, an early College Board member, remembered a time he spent in the local hospital:

> *"I was in the hospital this last summer and I had some of the finest nurses I've ever had in my life; in fact, I'm trying to figure out what kind of Christmas presents to buy them. They all graduated in the first class (at SWOC (sic))."*

The nursing program at the College remains the oldest continuous degree program on campus. When Ms. Barbara Davey took over the program in 1976 there were two separate, but concurrent nursing degree courses offered – one leading to the Practical Nursing degree and one leading to an Associate of Science degree in nursing. The nursing "lab" was in an old metal building about where Sumner Hall is located today and as Ms. Davey explained:

> *"...when we went into the lab to practice bathing an infant and it was raining outside, the roof leaked so badly that I would jokingly say to the students 'here is the shower to use!'"*

Since the Oregon State Board of Nursing had to approve the curriculum at SWOCC for both the Registered Nursing (RN) program and the Learning Practical Nursing (LPN) program, it took a while for both to be recognized. Once the LPN program was approved, students could enroll in the RN program, obtain their LPN certification, work in the local hospital (for higher pay), while they completed the course work for the higher degree. The nursing program continued to grow and today a student can not only obtain an Associate's degree in nursing, but also a Bachelor of Science degree from Oregon Health & Science University through an articulation program whereby they take all their course work on the SWOCC campus. A win for all involved.

The future seems bright for the nursing program at SWOCC. Two years ago it opened an "online" Associate's program on the Brookings campus. Lectures are a live video feed and lab work is conducted at the Good Samaritan long-term care facility in Brookings. In 2010, the College started another online nursing cohort in Coquille. The local high school generously provided two rooms for lab work; the clinical work is conducted under supervision at the Coquille Hospital.

Graduating Class of 1972.

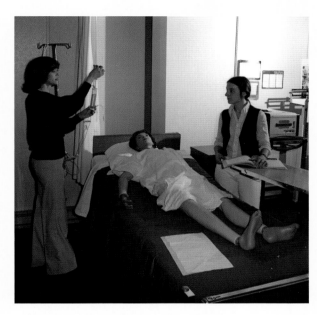

Nursing instruction in a simulation room – 1981.

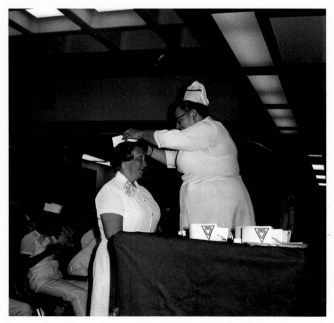

Nurse Isabelle LaFond places a nurse's graduation "cap" signaling the completion of the nursing course at SWOCC and a pin recognizing that achievement.

Another successful vocational program offered in the early years at SWOCC involved forestry. The federally financed College forest-aide training program began at the College in 1963 under the Manpower Development and Training Act of 1962; that year, 23 men enrolled in the program. The instructor was Warren Hootman, a local forester and surveyor. The forestry classes were also held at the Michigan Avenue School. Laboratory work was everywhere outdoors and foresters from the local timber companies lent a hand whenever asked. Students were screened by the Oregon Employment Department and came from all over the State to attend the 52-week long program. Over the years, the forestry program grew on campus as the demand for two-year college trained forestry technicians increased during the 1970s and early '80s when three professors handled the workload. At one time there were over 50 students enrolled in the program. The forestry program began to dwindle in response to the decline in local jobs within the timber industry and the program was finally dropped in the mid-'90s.

Forestry class on a field trip – ca 1963.

Forestry class learning how logging is done in the region using a model spar tree.

Almost from the very beginning, the Board of Education and Dr. Van Loan began thinking about a single campus for the College. The Board requested help from Salem and a survey team from the State Board of Higher Education reviewed several potential sites within Coos County that might be suitable for the new college campus. A lot of politics surfaced among the various town locations as they all vied for the College to be located within their jurisdiction.

Proposed site for the SWOCC campus by the City of North Bend.

Airport

Curry SWOCC Campus

Alternative site for SWOCC campus proposed by the Chamber of Commerce - 50 acres - 1961.

The City of North Bend, for instance, offered a 160-acre parcel known as the Coldiron property at Airport Heights. Another possibility was a 50-acre site where the current North Bend Bi-Mart Shopping Center is located. In those days, that area was called "dead man's curve" – probably relating to the road curving from Broadway onto Newmark.

Coos Bay offered a site in the Englewood region of town known as the Humbert tract. The City of Coquille also offered a very promising site for the campus that overlooked the Coquille Valley. The town of Empire offered a site that seemed the most logical due to the mere fact that the student population was concentrated in that area. (Even though Empire merged with the City of Coos Bay years later, it is still referred to as Empire today.) The team's final recommendation was the Empire Lakes location in Empire, the current home of the SWOCC main campus.

At the Board meeting on January 8, 1962 the decision was finalized; the new campus would be located at Empire Lakes (Bill Jordon made the motion and Bob Adams seconded. All directors voted in favor except for Henry Hansen who voted no [63]): 54.8 acres of land was gifted from the City of Empire; 35.4 acres of land was purchased from Mullen-Shiver for $30,000; and a year later, the Board purchased 35 acres from the Queens family. To complete the final ownership, in 1965 the City of Coos Bay sold to the College an island at Empire Lakes for $5,000. The total area that comprised the original campus site was 125 acres.

But according to Henry Hansen,

> *"Empire Lakes was the most worthless piece of property they* (Empire City) *had."* [15]

Harvey Crim, the first business manager at SWOCC, commented,

"It was a miserable place to get into. You couldn't see the cotton-picking thing because the underbrush was about 10 feet high. The first time Dr. Van Loan brought me here, we walked down a blazed trail, and you couldn't tell anything was here until you stepped into the lake. Massive brush and mud holes is about what it was." [77]

Undoubtedly, they were referring to the damp and swampy land that surrounded the lakes and the amount of old stumps and logs on the shoreline. The location needed an extensive engineering network of underground drainage pipes to handle the wet environment. The area was also covered by a thick undergrowth of brush and trees that came in after a fire in 1939 that burned the surrounding spruce forest, all of which added considerable expense as the campus was literally carved out of a forest.

Looking back even farther in time, Don Stensland, geology professor at the College, commented on the geology of Empire Lakes:

"The lakes were created by inter-dunal basins where water from the surrounding drainage and rainfall are trapped by both a hard pan and older dune deposits. Underlying all the dune systems along the coast is a marine terrace deposit of Pleistocene Age. The dunes are formed by sands transported to the coastal regions by rivers, the most important of which is the Columbia River. Ocean currents move the eroded material up and down the coast. Onshore winds pick up the dried sand and move it inland, eventually forming great dune sheets which trap water and form lakes." [13]

Surveying at the Empire Lakes site in 1961.

Adding additional flavor to the history of Empire Lakes' site, John Topits, a local businessman from Empire, said:

"These lakes were used for water by Empire City as early as 1859. A cedar lined pipe transported the water to the City. The middle lake was dammed to seal the outlet and raise the level of the lake by five feet to improve the pressure delivered to the City. Around 1900, the lower lake was dammed with concrete and its level was also raised by five feet. The National Guard helped dredge the lake and clean it out for a swimming area at that time. A spillway on both the middle and lower lakes keeps the depth at 16 feet..." [13]

The lakes were also used for industrial power. In 1883, for instance, the Oregon Southern Improvement Company built the largest saw mill on the West Coast at the time and the water for their steam boilers was piped from the middle Empire Lake to the mill. The lakes continued to supply water to the area until 1956 when the Coos Bay – North Bend Water Board began supplying the area with potable water. [14]

Even President Dr. Wendell Van Loan got into the act of surveying his college turf.

Aerial view of Empire Lakes –
ca mid 1950s.

Looking south across Empire Lakes to where
the SWOCC campus will eventually be built.
The Georgia Pacific wigwam burner can be
seen belching smoke in the background.

Dr. Wendell Van Loan and Jack
Brookins looking over Empire
Lake ca – 1963.

In 1972, the community and students came
together to clean the logs and debris from
Empire Lake.

This is only a portion of the accumulation
of logs, litter and debris that was among
the junk removed from Empire Lakes in
an effort to beautify and un-pollute the
lake. The project was sponsored by the
Coos Bay-North Bend Rotary Club and
local businesses, with a donated yarder,
trucks and other equipment used. There
were over 100 volunteers, including
loggers, businessmen, Boy Scouts,
National Guard, SWOCC students and
staff members. The volunteers labored for
two long days before they were satisfied
with their work.

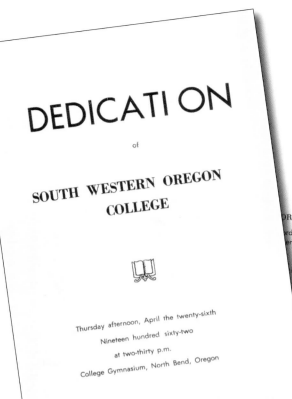

DEDICATION

of

SOUTH WESTERN OREGON COLLEGE

Thursday afternoon, April the twenty-sixth
Nineteen hundred sixty-two
at two-thirty p.m.
College Gymnasium, North Bend, Oregon

BUDGET COMMITTEE

...rdan   A. P. Stinchfield   Robert A. Schulze
...ertson   Calvin McAlister   Maurice Engelgau
*Pat Masterson

...ATION COMMITTEE

...W. Slover   Frances McKenzie
...A. R. Chidwick   Ellamae Judges

...torney   James Bailey,   Accountant

...CULTY

Curtis, William
Eickworth, Clara M.
Ellis, Eugene
Ferguson, Helen
Gamble, William
Godard, Harold
Gross, Charlie
Hartley, David
Heckard, Calvin
Holmes, Josephine
Holmes, William J.
Humphrey, Thomas
Karl, Maggie
Kilby, James
King, Jessie
Leegard, Ellsworth L.

Merrill, Osmond
Moffitt, Donald
Morse, Don
Neilson, Ursula
Orr, William
Osborne, Elizabeth
Osborne, Robert
Oylear, Chester
Popp, Janice
Romig, Maurice
Salisbury, Robert
Shibley, Lyle
Smith, Robert
Spaugh, Roger
Stender, Veneita
Stoll, Eli E.
Trembley, David L.
Trussell, Margaret
Ulett, Gerald
Van Loan, Lillian
Van Loan, Wendell
Van Ryckevorsel, Elisabeth
Whitney, Larry
Willard, Theodore

PROGRAM

Mr. Henry F. Hansen *Chairman of the Board of Directors*	Presiding
761st Radar Squadron Color Guard *North Bend Air Force Base*	Presentation of Colors
North Bend High School Band *Leo Howley, Director*	"The Star Spangled Banner" The National Anthem
Rev. A. Robert Chidwick *Rector, Episcopal Church, Coquille*	Invocation
Messrs. Orville A. Adams, G. E. Albertson, W. A. Jordan, Leslie King	Presentation of Directors
Dr. J. W. Sherburne *Dean of General Extension Division*	Presentation of Representatives of State System of Higher Education
Dr. Charles D. Byrne *Chancellor Emeritus*	
Mr. William E. Walsh *Chairman State Board of Higher Education*	
North Bend High School Band	"Highlights from Camelot" Lerner and Loewe
Mr. William C. Loomis *Director of Community Colleges and Industrial Education*	Presentation of Representatives of State Board of Education
Mr. Oscar Paulson *Ass't. Supt. Vocational Education*	
Dr. Leon P. Minear *State Superintendent of Public Instruction*	
Mr. Robert C. Croft *Director Collegiate Division*	Representatives of the Administration and Faculty Division of South Western Oregon College
Mr. Maurice M. Romig *Director Technical-Vocational and Adult Division*	
Dr. Wendell L. Van Loan *President South Western Oregon College*	
North Bend High School Band	"Harvest Home" — Yoder

The College Board of Education continued to push forward as the community demands for advanced and technical training were growing. The branch office of the architectural firm of Skidmore, Owings and Merrill in Portland was hired to develop a Master Plan for the new campus. The firm presented their final comprehensive design to the Board in March 1963. It envisioned the campus being built-out over time in five separate phases.

The architect's original rendering of the SWOCC campus as presented to the College Board of Education in 1962.

Construction Begins

The clearing and grading portion of Phase 1 at Empire Lakes started in May 1963 in preparation for constructing the first two buildings on the new campus. Throughout its 50-year history, each time an expansion was undertaken, the ubiquitous water, mud, brush, stumps and trees were obstacles that had to be overcome. Donald W. Thompson was awarded the contract for constructing the first two buildings on the campus for a bid price of $300,180. The footings were poured that same fall and students began occupying the two new buildings in the spring of 1964.

Construction begins on the new campus in the spring of 1963.

Dr. Van Loan explains where the new access road needs to go to operator Bob Angel – May 1963.

The firm of Skidmore, Owings and Merrill were the architects who designed the Master Plan for constructing the SWOCC campus. Donald W. Thompson was the general contractor for Phase 1 of the project.

Brush and stumps were everywhere and had to be disposed
of by whatever manner was
feasible. Here a crane piles and
re-piles the debris in order to
separate the wood from the dirt
in 1963. It probably smoldered
for weeks!

Construction continued with
the clearing of the trees and
underbrush.

A college campus will rise from
the forest and swampland.

Water was everywhere and
the mud was deep and sticky
– 1963.

Randolph Hall – classrooms

Umpqua Hall – shop classrooms

Dellwood Hall – ca 1966

Umpqua Hall – ca 1972

Students in the Automotive Technology classes in Umpqua Hall.

As the first two buildings were under construction, a "Name the Buildings Committee" was formed on campus. It was clear that the committee was not going to follow tradition and name the buildings after famous (or infamous) people or U.S. presidents, but rather something non-political. Some thought the buildings should be named after Native American tribes. The committee finally settled on naming the buildings after the old post offices that were no longer operational in Coos County.

The first two buildings to be constructed under the Master Plan were Umpqua and Randolph Halls. Randolph Hall would be for academic classroom work, while Umpqua Hall would be for vocational teaching.

The welding corner inside Fairview Hall.

The teachers and students had several unusual obstacles to overcome during the early phases of building the campus. The winter rains made the trails between the graveled (or not!) parking lot and classroom muddy and slippery. Even though buildings were completed in 1964, the College still used the other old classroom sites off campus. During those years, schedules had to be planned such that sufficient time was allowed for a student or faculty member to travel from the Empire Lakes campus class to another class being held at the Airport, Michigan Avenue Elementary School or other building still under lease by the College.

The "mud bowl" was the unfinished parking lot behind Tioga Hall as it was affectionately called. The Southwester 10/28/71

Umpqua Hall

Dellwood Hall

An aerial view of the Southwestern Oregon Community College Campus with Phase 1 completed – 1964. The only buildings completed at the time were Randolph and Umpqua Halls and the south parking lot (Parking Lot #1). It would be several decades before the trees and brush were cleared and the completed campus and parking lots emerged from the surrounding forest.

State of Oregon
CHARTER

Know all men by these presents that:

South Western Oregon College

was established by vote of the people on May 1, 1961

under the authority and by virtue of the laws of the sovereign State of Oregon, and is hereby granted all rights and privileges arising therefrom and pertaining thereto.

In witness whereof, I have hereunto set my hand and have caused the Great Seal of the State of Oregon to be affixed this **13th** *day of* **October** *1964*

SWOCC was granted its official Charter by Governor Mark Hatfield on October 13,1964. However, there was a short, but political story between the time the College opened in September 1961 and the granting of the Charter.

Apparently some of the professors wanted to publish a catalog about the course offerings in that first term. Bob Croft, Ron Lilienthal and Don Moffitt worked on the catalog over the summer and inserted the statement that SWOC (sic) was an accredited institution – meaning college level transcripts could be transferred to any four-year college or institution.

Since the Northwest Association of Secondary and Higher Schools had not reviewed the course outlines or the credentials of the faculty, SWOC (sic) could not have been an accredited institution. That fall, the Chancellor came out in a news story stating that Southwestern Oregon College (sic) was not an accredited institution. One can imagine that the community and future students were in an uproar about the issues of accreditation. Fortunately, there was a State committee of professors from different colleges that reviewed the College's courses and approved them as transfer credits to their institutions. Problem solved!

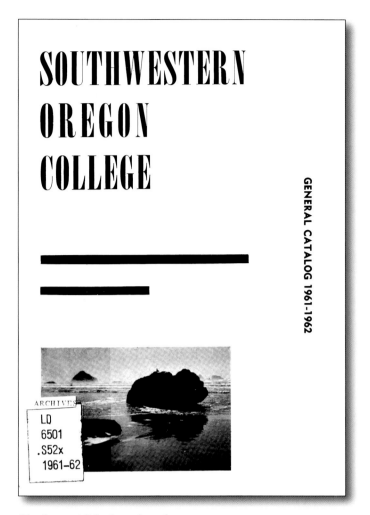

SOUTHWESTERN OREGON COLLEGE

GENERAL CATALOG 1961-1962

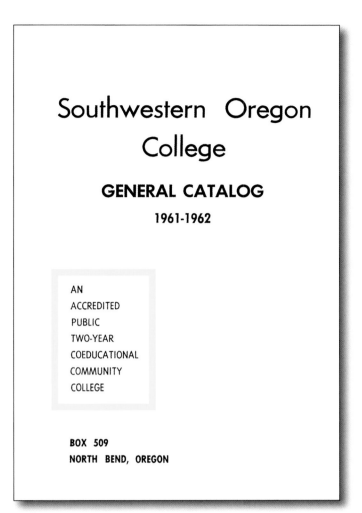

Southwestern Oregon College

GENERAL CATALOG

1961-1962

AN
ACCREDITED
PUBLIC
TWO-YEAR
COEDUCATIONAL
COMMUNITY
COLLEGE

BOX 509
NORTH BEND, OREGON

The first published catalog of classes showing the erroneous claim of accreditation.

Ms. Ferguson recalled what it was like that first year on the Empire Lakes campus:

> "I can remember parking my car in the parking lot; there was no surfacing done on the parking lot. I remember pulling out a pair of boots to walk through the muddy pathways from the parking lot to the building. I was so sold on having a new campus that I didn't mind the muddy sidewalks. I also recall teaching a class in Randolph Hall when Dellwood Hall was under construction and the jackhammers outside the door were so loud that I would have to stop talking until the noise stopped."

Pete Sorensen recalled the early campus in 1963 (he was 12 years of age):

> "There was a lot of mud everywhere."

Another fact that Sorensen recalled his father discussing had to do with a consultant's report:

> "Apparently the consultant noted that because the campus was situated some distance back from the City street and was surrounded by trees that if they left the lights on 24 hours per day, that they would have less vandalism. At night the whole place was all lit up!"

Another of the early instructors at the College who came to Coos Bay around the time Henry Hansen was getting the legislation passed for a new district was Veneita Stender. She had graduated from the University of Idaho with a teaching certificate in home economics. After taking a course in the home of Mrs. Clara Eickworth in Empire on a special sewing technique and studying the Bishop method of sewing, she was ready to teach clothing construction at the College.

Ms. Stender remembered very clearly what it was like to reach her classroom in Dellwood Hall from the parking lot on the new SWOCC campus:

> "There were no sidewalks during those first years on campus. Everyone had the same problem. We all came to class with muddy boots and changed into regular shoes only to have to put the boots back on to attend another class in Dellwood Hall or return to their automobiles. It was also dark on campus. They didn't have all the nice lighting they have today, so it was often a dark and rainy evening when I walked back to my car after class."

As the first parking lot on the Empire Lakes site was being built, the students, faculty, and administrators parked their cars wherever they could find space. While the faculty tended to get the preferred spots, the students parked wherever they could find an open spot, which often resulted in their car getting mired in the mud. [61]

Ms. Helen Ferguson's secretarial science class -1967.

What about the classroom and equipment on the new campus? Ms. Ferguson responded to the interviewer:

"We had excellent ones. We had an excellent typing lab the first time we put one together. And then a few years later when we added a second typing lab, Jack Brookins went to bat for me when I stressed a particular brand of typewriter that I felt was going to be superior as far as an instructional tool was concerned. It represented more of a financial outlay than some people felt we needed, but we ended up with a second typing lab that has continued to serve us beautifully." [43]

Ms. Ferguson went on to discuss the type of students that attended SWOC (sic) during those first couple of years. She said they were pioneers, just like the instructors. There was an active student body that worked in concert with the faculty and administration as everyone tried to work out the "kinks" and challenges of starting a college in multiple locations. The faculty acted as a single unit through what was called the SWOC (sic) Faculty Club which later became the Faculty Senate after a constitution was written and Ben Fawver became its president. The faculty was small and out of necessity had to work together to make things happen – as Ms. Ferguson indicated several times throughout the interview:

"There was also a strong social bond among the faculty in those early years as if the success of the College rested on our shoulders. As the campus grew in size and complexity, the communication and camaraderie seemed to fade." [46]

As the students began showing up for class on the new Empire Lakes campus, some of the locals became curious as to what might be available for them. Since this was a community college, they were part of the community – weren't they?

At first some of the local wildlife were curious about their new neighbors and could be seen prowling the campus looking for handouts from student lunches. Rabbits could be seen scurrying back to the protective cover of the surrounding brush.

Like all students, some needed a little discipline and training in group dynamics!

In addition to the wild critters that frequented the campus, there were a group of chickens that greeted the students during the early 1970s. Apparently the first member of the SWOCC chicken family was a colorful rooster that was left on campus after an Easter holiday in 1970. As the story goes, one morning the assistant superintendent of buildings, Mr. Jack Cabrera, was raising the flag when he heard a rooster crowing from high in a tree. He started feeding it, but felt the lone chicken needed company, so he put an ad in the newspaper on behalf of the lonely male and soon three hens were donated by a woman from Hauser. From this auspicious beginning the flock of chickens began to multiply until the College mascot recognized the opportunity for an easy meal. The local raccoons, skunks, cats, dogs, and children reduced the chicken population to zero. So the campus was free of fowl; that was until five Bantam chickens were given to the College. At the time, chicken feed went from $2.65 per 50-pound sack to $6 and the College simply could not afford to award such expensive scholarships any longer. Just like in a Disney story, this turn of events indeed had a happy ending. A young student at the College took the flock home one day, where a newly built pen was awaiting them and they lived out their days in a tranquil city home.

It didn't take long before the neighbors felt right at home and some even tried to acquire a book or two at the library.

Looking at the above photos,
one must wonder who is the
college graduate?

Ms. Barbara Dodrill, who before returning to SWOCC after getting her Master's degree from Oregon State University, remembered taking business classes from Ms. Ferguson on Marshfield High School's temporary college campus. Ms. Dodrill attended SWOC (sic) for two years, but never graduated, because they required a couple of terms of Physical Education classes. According to Ms. Dodrill, "I didn't have time for P.E. in my life and I told them if I don't know enough by age 40 to exercise, I'm not ever going to learn!" So, she never got a degree from SWOCC, but returned to the campus in 1972 as a visiting instructor and eventually became a tenured professor. Aside from a 10-year hiatus, she taught in the business department until retiring in 2003.

With wind in their sails, at the January 1964 meeting the College Board of Education authorized the start of construction of Phase II of the Master Plan. This phase included a classroom building, laboratory building, and an administrative building. Murphy Construction won this bid and began work in October of that same year. The manner in which the campus was designed allowed for the preservation of as much of the natural setting as possible. The Board also authorized renovation work to be done on the old Naval facility still under lease at the North Bend Airport.

When Jack Brookins became president in 1965, he recognized the need to provide women with a way to broaden their skills. Ms. Stender suggested that one of the things that would give women a way to contribute to the economy of their home was to learn how to make their own clothing as well as that for their children. She was immediately employed as a full-time vocational teacher to meet the need of teaching clothing construction, and in 1965 she taught her first course in Randolph Hall. She said her class size was around 20 women ranging in age from the mid-20s to over 50.

Ms. Stender remarked in an interview that the College was always looking for ways to help women expand their education, and her class in clothing construction was one example. As she explained, there was full employment in the area at the time and the man's salary was sufficient to support the family. There were few opportunities for women to work outside the home; teaching, medical and clerical jobs were just about the limit of employment options for women.

The home economics course taught by Veneita Stender ca 1964. The space obviously did double duty as a science classroom.

During the first formative years of the community colleges across the State of Oregon, there developed a tension between the two-year colleges and the larger four-year institutions regarding qualifications of faculty and course content taught in the lower division transfer courses. This tension apparently involved the perceived threat that the community colleges were in some way attracting students who could have gone from a high school directly to the university vs. spending their first two years at the community college. However, it did not take long for both the University of Oregon and Oregon State University to realize that the community colleges were excellent reservoirs for recruitment as the community colleges could "weed out" the students who did not want to pursue a four-year program and/or were not ready for college level work. This led to a smoother relationship as each level of post-secondary education cooperated in a manner that provided a relatively seamless transition from the community colleges upwards to the universities.

As a sign of the strengthening relationship between the post-secondary colleges, on January 23, 1966, the College held a dedication ceremony to commemorate the completion of Phase II of the Master Plan for the SWOCC campus. Dr. John R. Howard, president of Lewis and Clark College, was the keynote speaker and he remarked:

> "The people who are educated in schools of higher learning, of which SWOCC is one, are the ones to whom the world is looking to solve its present day problems such as war, race, poverty, urbanization and lack of moral conviction. In this age of war (the Vietnam war) there is no logical alternative to mediation…the problems made by ordinary men will have to be resolved by extraordinary men."

As the student body began to form on the new campus, it put forth some rules as to how the students were expected to act. The Board approved the Student Code of Conduct that was first published in the SWOCC Student Handbook in 1965 [36]:

This college is dedicated not only to learning and advancement of knowledge, but also to the development of ethically sensitive and responsible persons. It seeks to achieve these goals through a sound educational program and policies governing student conduct that encourages independence and maturity. Students are expected to conduct themselves as mature young men and women. Please note the following:

1. Recognizes the rights of others – in the library, classrooms, lounges and parking areas. Congregating outside and other unnecessary disruptions of classes is prohibited.

2. The possession or use of alcoholic beverages on school property is prohibited. The same regulation applies to off-campus events under school sponsorship.

3. Smoking is not permitted in classrooms, shops, gymnasium or library. Students may smoke in the lounges, halls or outside campus buildings.

4. Gambling is prohibited by law in the State of Oregon. Students gambling will be subject to expulsion and penalties of State law.

5. The student lounges are places for students to relax. When smoking use ash trays. Use proper receptacles for all waste paper.

That is not to say that women studying for transfer credits at SWOCC were not exposed to some of the traditional "icky" biology lab work! Here Professor Ben Fawver guides two female students through the intricacies of dissecting a crayfish.

In those early years, there were not many extra curricular activities on the SWOCC campus. Two local service clubs had a campus wing – the Circle K from the Kiwanis organization for men and Golden Z from the Zonta organization for women. There were only three options for intercollegiate sports – men's basketball, played in the old Navy gym; track, where the performance was a little better as the Lakers set seven state records; and wrestling, where five men made up the team.

It is important to pause here and reflect on what was going on in the nation, Oregon and our community at the time SWOC (sic) opened its doors in the fall of 1961. The baby boom generation (born from 1946 – 1964) had yet to reach college age when the College started, but would begin graduating from high school as early as 1964; the 77-million strong wave of young people would soon be looking for additional education and SWOCC would have to adapt and grow.

The country as a whole was under the dark shadow of fear from atomic annihilation as the "Cold War" heated up; extreme social unrest gripped the nation. The Berlin Wall was built and Star Trek created a whole new cult. Johnny Carson's Tonight Show started and had a 30-year successful run on television. Rachel Carson's book, Silent Spring, sounded the alarm that would launch the environmental movement across America. And Oregon passed the acceptance of Daylight Savings in 1962. The minimum wage during the '60s was a mere $1 per hour.

John F. Kennedy gave his famous quote in his inauguration speech: "Ask not what your country can do for you - ask what you can do for your country." Three months into his new administration the young U.S. president would be tested when he ordered the Bay of Pigs invasion in an unsuccessful attempt to overthrow the new Cuban government headed by Fidel Castro. He would be tested again during the Cuban missile crisis and the capture of Gary Powers in his U-2 spy plane that was shot down over Soviet air space. Nikita Khrushchev would remove his shoe at the United Nation's Assembly and pound it unceremoniously on the table in defiance. Meanwhile, Uri Gagarin became the first man to reach "space" in the Russian craft Vostok 1 and President Kennedy vowed to put an American on the moon by the end of the decade. Unfortunately, Kennedy never lived to see Neil Armstrong climb down the ladder and say in broken transmission back to earth: "That's one small step for man, one giant leap for mankind."

President Kennedy would fall to an assassin's bullet fired by Lee Harvey Oswald on November 22, 1963. Those still living today probably recall exactly where they were when the news of his death came over the airways. (SWOCC closed its campus from the date of Kennedy's death until his funeral.) Jack Ruby killed Oswald as Oswald was being transported to a new holding facility. Robert Kennedy, the president's brother, would also fall to an assassin's bullet five years later, and younger brother Senator Edward Kennedy was arrested for leaving the scene of an accident at Chappaquiddick. Harvey Crim, the business manager at the College from 1963 to 1989, said when Robert Kennedy visited the SWOCC campus shortly before he was assassinated in San Francisco, a huge turnout came on campus to hear him speak. It was a "real big deal for our little college," Crim added.

Martin Luther King, Jr. gave his famous "I Have a Dream" speech and 200,000 people marched on Washington, D.C. demanding equal rights for blacks. The Civil Rights Act of 1964 and The Voting Rights Act of 1965 changed the lives of African Americans and other minorities by insuring equal rights on paper, but not on the streets of America. King would be assassinated in 1968, setting off extensive race riots across the country, especially in Watts, California and Newark, New Jersey.

The Tonkin Gulf (Vietnam War) incident began in the summer of 1964 and a full scale war erupted that continued well into the next decade. This would test the fabric of America as serious clashes on college campuses occurred as the military draft swung into high gear. Cassius Clay, or Muhammad Ali as he was later known, would become an icon in the sports world along with his court cases protecting his religious rights to not be drafted into the military. On October

15, 1969, the Associated Student Government (ASG) at SWOCC supported the Vietnam Moratorium on stopping the war, and demonstrations were held on college campuses nationwide. As far as other civil demonstrations on the campus, there were not many.

The fashion and various hairstyles on the SWOCC campus of the 1960s.

In essence, the country was on high alert status throughout the entire decade.

As for fashions, the 1960s decade began with men in crew cuts and women with bouffant hairstyles. As the decade progressed, the hair on men got longer and hairstyles for women were either short on some or straight and long on others to mimic their favorite celebrities. Hot pants and miniskirts shocked the older generation. Chubby Checker would start a whole new dance craze starting with the Twist, as co-eds invented new ways to interpret other music with the Stomp, the Swim, the Monkey, the Watusi, the Funky Chicken, and the Mashed Potato; folk music dominated college campuses near the end of the decade. The Beverly Hillbillies would find oil in their backyard in the Ozarks and move to Beverly Hills, and Goldie Hawn debuted on Laugh-In.

The cross streets of Haight-Ashbury became famous for the hippie movement that found acceptance in the younger generation as social unrest stunned the country; it epitomized the culture clash that was stirring in the nation. Respect for authority declined among the youth, and minor crime rates soared. The antiestablishment hippie movement endorsed drugs, rock music, mystic religions and sexual freedom as evidenced by the 500,000 who were filmed in attendance at the Woodstock Festival in Bethel, New York. Marijuana was widely used on college campuses, but condemned by society at large. The well known Harvard psychologist, Timothy Leary, encouraged the use of LSD as a mind-opening drug.

Some common language of the 1960s: [31]

To bag –	to steal
To beat feet –	to leave in a hurry
Blitzed –	drunk
Bone yard –	auto wrecking yard
To bug –	to bother or irritate
Cherry –	perfect or pristine
Church key –	beer can opener
Dig –	to understand
Crash –	go to bed
Groady –	grotesque
Jam –	party
Meat –	a guy
To moon –	to drop one's pants to expose one's backside (butt)
Old lady –	mother
Old man –	father
To scarf –	to eat fast
To split –	to leave
Threads –	clothes

Sports fans watched Roger Maris break Babe Ruth's home run record, and baseball idols such as Mickey Mantle, Yogi Berra, Willie Mays and Sandy Koufax added to the aura of the game. Jackie Robinson was inducted into the Baseball Hall of Fame – the first black player to be admitted. Wilt Chamberlain and Bill Russell would dominate the game of basketball. Y.A. Tittle and R.C. Owens of the San Francisco 49ers perfected the "Alley Oop" pass in football while Johnnie Unitas and Bart Starr would lead their respective teams to championships.

As far as technology is concerned, and from the perspective of 50 years into the future, the 1960s were pretty mundane. Big Blue (IBM) dominated the computer industry and had converted from the vacuum tube technology to the integrated circuits. Hewlett-Packard entered the industry with their HP-2116 unit. BASIC and FORTRAN, with their ubiquitous punch cards, were the computer language of the day. Probably the most controversial technological invention of the time was the portable calculator devised by Texas Instruments. Controversial, at least in the minds of parents, because many adults believed children should learn the basics of math – long division and multiplication tables - rather than simply relying on the calculator key strokes to perform the work. The audio cassette tape recorder was also invented during the '60s along with an artificial heart pump and a practical barcode system. The first automatic bank teller machine – ATM – was put into service in 1969. Given the risk of jumping ahead in the story about SWOCC, another debate is

Students in the business classes at SWOCC in those early days had to learn how to use modern calculators and typewriters.

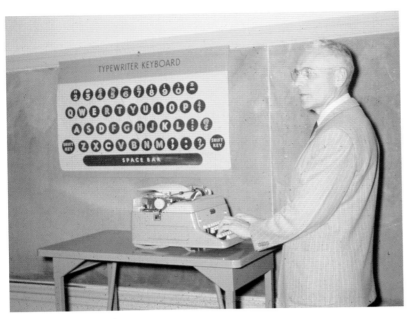 

Teaching typing in the 1960s.

now occurring concerning writing skills. At least one of the elementary schools within the College district no longer teaches cursive but instead teaches computer keyboarding skills. The presumption here in 2011 is that students will no longer write by hand, but will do all their communication on keyboards of all sizes!

Locally, these national trends and political issues seemed far away from the conservative logging communities of southwestern Oregon and the SWOCC campus. Several interviews were conducted for this book with students and instructors who were at SWOCC during the latter part of the decade. Without exception, all reported that there was very little evidence on campus of radical demonstrations that were so prevalent on the larger universities throughout the nation. There were undoubtedly a few debates about the Vietnam War and several articles were written in *The Southwester* about the War, but in general things were pretty quiet.

As far as the local economy was concerned, things were on the move in the forest products industry in southwestern Oregon. In 1961, the Menasha Corporation was building a new paper mill at Jordon Cove; this was in addition to a plywood plant the company was operating in North Bend. Weyerhaeuser Company had a huge integrated wood products complex along the bay front where The Mill Casino now stands. Georgia Pacific was operating a large saw-mill and plywood mill complex at the south end of Coos Bay and just across the Isthmus Slough was the plywood mill of Coos Head. The large national forest products corporations were certainly in play within the College district.

The Moore Mill and Lumber Company was running a large sawmill in Bandon, and one in Empire. Roseburg Lumber Company was operating a large plywood plant in Coquille, as was Georgia Pacific. Other smaller sawmills were scattered from Reedsport to Brookings to take advantage of the timber in the region. Rail service reaching from Powers to the main lines in Eugene allowed freight to be hauled at a competitive rate to inland markets. However, the major mode of transportation for the forest products was by water.

#5.
Vessels loading lumber
at Georgia-Pacific Corp.
and Portland Docks
Coos Bay, Oregon

#9. Hillstrom Dock
Mill "B" Dock
North Bend City Dock

#4.
Ship loading lumber at
Weyerhaeuser Co. Dock
North Bend, Oregon

#6.
Coos Bay Pulp Corp.
Empire, Oregon

Beginning in the early part of the twentieth century, the shipping channel in Coos Bay provided superb transportation advantages for moving timber products out of Coos and western Douglas counties. The above photographs document some of the milling facilities adjacent to the shipping channel in Coos Bay. Aside from the spotty recessions, the timber industry was the backbone of the economy of southwestern Oregon for over a century. Today, the industry is a small shadow of its original self. Photos courtesy of the University of Oregon.

On October 12, 1962, typhoon Frieda made landfall at Cape Blanco along the southern Oregon coast with sustained winds of 150 mph and gusts up to 180 mph. It became known nationwide as the Columbus Day Storm. The devastation caused by the storm was horrific and the amount of timber uprooted or broken off throughout Coos, western Douglas, and Curry counties was unfathomable. Once the damage was assessed, the amount of timber lying on the ground was more that the local mills could consume before it would rot or start an insect epidemic.

The U.S. Government traveled to Japan to ask for their assistance in purchasing some of the damaged timber for use in their mills and country. After a couple of trial log shipments, the Japanese demand for Douglas Fir logs exploded and Coos Bay quickly became the "world's largest forest products exporting port" – a position they maintained for the next 30 years.

The Ken Ann Maru loaded with Douglas Fir logs heading for Japan from Coos Bay.

The point to note here is that not only were the mills within SWOCC's district boundaries at full employment during the '60s, the extra push caused by the Columbus Day Storm in 1962 created a hyper-employment situation as loggers rushed to remove the down timber and new employees, families and contractors flooded into the area. All of this boded well for passing operating levies for the College as enrollment on campus tripled over the decade. And the forestry technician program could not produce enough graduates fast enough!

About the time that SWOCC undertook construction of Phase III of the Master Plan, the economic tide that had been so favorable for the forest products industry was about to change. In response to ever growing pressure from the environmental movement across the country, the federal government began reassessing its policies regarding timber harvests on public lands vs. setting aside large areas for wilderness protection - primarily in the western part of the nation. This debate raged for years; more and more lands were set aside for wilderness use and competition for a shrinking source of timber drove prices of logs for the local sawmills skyward. This caused many of the less efficient, older mills to close and employment to fall.

As the Congressional decisions regarding these forests unfolded over the next 20 years, the impact on the west - and particularly Coos Bay - would prove disastrous. The Wilderness Act of 1964 and the Endangered Species Act passed a decade later probably had a greater impact on the lives of the people within the SWOCC district than any other Congressional action before or since. As the old adage goes: "Your life is not safe when Congress is in session."

While forest products was the dominant industry in southwestern Oregon during the twentieth century, fishing and dairying were extremely important to the local economy and ranked number two and three in the region. Numerous fish processing plants were in operation in Charleston, off-loading salmon, shrimp and rock fish caught by the sizable fishing fleets working out of Coos Bay, Winchester Bay and Bandon. Hughes Air West provided excellent air service to transport fish products to the inland markets. But the fishing industry would succumb to policy decisions - similar to those impacting the forest products industry - made in Washington, D.C. Congress and the federal agencies that regulated the fishing industry began reducing the quota of fish being caught in the ocean just off the shores of Coos Bay.

Fortunately for the efforts of Henry Hansen and Jessie Laird, the major negative employment impacts discussed above would be some 15 years into the future – well past the major push by them to establish the College in 1961 or the major construction push initiated by Presidents Van Loan and Jack Brookins during the decade.

In 1965, Brookins took the reins from Dr. Van Loan as the second president at SWOCC and continued to expand the campus at Empire Lakes. Brookins would successfully lead the College for 20 years and experience the ebb and flow of voter acceptance or rejections of the operating levies for the College as the local economy began its decline. Undoubtedly frustrated at times, but in the tradition of those who preceded him and as an example for those who followed, Brookins would not be swayed from the vision of the College's founders.

From a construction point of view, there were interesting engineering challenges facing the expansion of the campus. Much of the campus property is located at the confluence of all the water that naturally drains off the surrounding hillsides and into the Empire Lakes. Buildings constructed anywhere near the lake or in a low spot on the campus had a significant water disposal problem to solve. In fact, there is a stream that runs year round through the campus and the original architect/engineers had to determine a way of channeling it through the property and into the lake.

Jack Brookins, president of Southwestern Oregon Community College 1965-1985.

Today, there is an intricate network of drainage pipes beneath the campus that transports the water to an aqueduct that flows through the campus and into the lake. At one spot, the engineers created an attractive cement structure that became known as the "Poet's Eye." According to John Speasl, Athletic Director, the space was designed so that a professor could stand on the pupil and deliver a lecture to their students sitting on the natural outdoor amphitheater. Still today, during warm days in late spring or early fall, professors can be found with their classes enjoying the spot.

Drainage canal running through campus.

Poet's Eye behind Dellwood Hall.

Sometimes the Poet's Eye was used for purposes other than an English lecture.

Wonder what class he teaches?

Another engineering problem faced by the original architects was how to deal with sewage that would be generated in every building on campus. Since the City's sewer lines were "up hill" from the main buildings, pumps had to be installed with more underground pipes to handle the effluent. Obviously the water drainage from the hillsides simply needed gravity to work, but if the sewer pumps failed, the campus was immediately closed – which happened more than once. As time went along, backup power systems were installed, so if power stoppage occurred, classes could continue.

President Brookins is credited with overseeing the completion of Phase II of the Master Plan in September 1965 - Dellwood (administration and library), Sitkum (classrooms) and Coaledo (science lab) Halls were all built between 1964 and 1965 at a total construction cost of $693,000.

Dellwood Hall construction

Sitkum Hall construction

Dellwood Hall

Sitkum Hall

An aerial view of the SWOCC campus following the completion of Phase II of the Master Plan 1965 – 1966. During the construction of Phase II, the Board of Directors decided to construct a student lounge – the first to be built on any community college in the State. However, as local industries were still recovering from an earlier recession, the ballot measure to build the lounge was defeated at the polls. However, the College decided to forge ahead with their plans to dedicate the profits from the bookstore, the vending machines and cafeteria toward the construction of the new student lounge. It took a few years, but sufficient funds were collected to build the first student lounge on any community college campus.

Student Lounge – 1965

The College continued to move forward under Brookins' leadership, providing an ever expanding list of courses – both transferrable and vocational. Several retired faculty members interviewed for this book remarked about the friendly environment they experienced during their first visit to the campus while being recruited. The campus culture was incredibly welcoming as the young professors searched for their first teaching jobs out of college – and many stayed at SWOCC until they retired 30 or 40 years later! Several remarked how much they liked the community and the potential of being part of building a new campus and academic programs, essentially from the ground up. Former English professor and retired dean of instruction Phill Anderson, for instance, recalled that when he and his family first moved to Coos Bay, several faculty women brought over casseroles for them as they were moving in. Apparently something like that was unheard of in the San Francisco area, from where the Andersons had just moved.

According to Ms. Dodrill:

> "Jack Brookins was so good for this college because he treated everyone with the same amount of dignity; whether they taught a transfer math course, a vocational accounting course or were a part-time faculty, everyone was on an equal footing. I recall that we had an advisory committee from the community for just about every vocational program offered."

The SWOCC campus as it appeared during the beginning of Phase III of the Master Plan. Randolph, Umpqua, Dellwood, Sitkum and Coaledo Halls were complete and Tioga and Prosper Halls were under construction ca 1967. Photo courtesy of Ward Robertson.

During the past 50 years, SWOCC has had a total of six presidents. From one perspective, Jack Brookins would serve the longest tenure as president and yet have the least amount of formal education as indicated by his credentials. While all the other presidents held a doctorate degree of some type, Brookins did not. He was brought to SWOCC as the dean of vocational education while he was working on his PhD at Berkley. In an investigative article in *The World* newspaper in 1980 about Brookins' contract with the College, there was some question about his contract containing a clause that he was to complete his doctorate degree within a certain period of time. Brookins told the paper, "…that was not a condition of my employment and not in my contract." Apparently he never found the time to finish it. Even so, he was the right leader for the College at the right time. His interest and background in vocational education was probably one of the reasons why SWOCC was known for its broad course offerings. When asked, he proudly said that he still had his pin from the carpenter's union.

The Carpentry class – 1967

Newmark Avenue

Not surprising, it was early in Brookins' tenure that a vocational program was started on campus that involved training for carpenters. The doors at the College were opened in the summer of 1967 to over 160 journeymen carpenters – the largest program for carpenters in the country at that time. The local carpentry unions in the region, in conjunction with the College, helped provide a program designed to assist apprentice and journeymen alike in adjusting to new skills and techniques. It was made available through the federal Manpower and Development Training Act. These carpentry courses were held every Saturday for 20 weeks. [8]

Like most community colleges throughout the nation, SWOCC has always been known as a commuter college – never having buses to transport students from their home to campus. When the two main parking lots on campus were being paved, traffic jams were common on Newmark Avenue.

As one story goes, even President Brookins stood guard at the campus entrance to direct students to where they were to park their cars during the paving of the College parking lots. Obviously, the residents in Empire and those who used Newmark Avenue had to be quite patient until the paving was completed and the students could resume parking their cars directly on campus property.

Phase III of the Master Plan was the most interesting and costly of all the building projects up to that time. It involved the two largest buildings on campus – Prosper Hall (the gymnasium) and Tioga Hall (the library and learning center). As envisioned by the original architects, the serene setting of Empire Lakes again played an important role in the design of Tioga Hall with its west-facing windows on the fifth floor overlooking the upper lake and "Lecture Island." Later, as part of Phase IV construction, Empire Hall would also benefit from the beauty overlooking the lake.

Since Prosper Hall was a gymnasium, the construction would require long beams that would span from wall to wall in order to provide space for basketball courts with room for bleachers. The engineers called for large wooden laminated beams – four feet thick and 140 feet long – to make the span. No one in town manufactured this type of engineered product. The beams were probably supplied by Columbia Manufacturing in Portland. This meant the beams (five in all) had to be trucked a long distance from the mill and maneuvered through the streets of Coos Bay – along with a police escort. A specially designed truck and trailer configuration were used to transport the beams to the site where a 45-ton crane would lift them into place.

Making the turn with a 140-foot beam used in the construction of Prosper Hall. A driver actually sat in the trailer beneath the back of the beam to maneuver the load around turns and sharp corners.

The design of Prosper Hall was unique. At the time of construction, there were only two other buildings like it across the nation – one at OIT and one at the Air Force Academy in Colorado Springs. Asked about the interior design of the gym, John Speasl noted that the mezzanine level in the SWOCC building was unique and a bit of an afterthought. The coaches' offices in other colleges with similar architecture were on the bottom floor providing access to all students, including those with handicaps. But Prosper Hall was originally built without an elevator, and in fact is smaller than the original design called for, due to rising cost of materials and managing the costs of construction within the requisite budget.

Today, there are elevators from the ground level to the basketball court level, but none to the mezzanine. Asked why the elevators were not extended to the "third floor" the answer seemed to be one of cost overruns during the original construction and "architectural balance" – to get an elevator to reach to the mezzanine level, a large box containing the upper mechanisms would have to have been built on one side of the roof. Apparently, that was unacceptable, but in the words of the current generation, "a little lame!"

Two cranes were required to set the beams in place.

Laying the specially designed hardwood floor inside Prosper Hall.

Prosper Hall – 1967

The other building constructed under Phase III of the Master Plan was Tioga Hall, or as it was originally called, "the Learning Center." It was designed to be built in two stages. Stage 1 involved building the first two floors. The Robert D. Morrow Construction Company of Salem undertook the project. Stage 1 was completed throughout the winter of 1966-67 with minimal disruption to campus life. During the summer of 1967, and before construction began on Stage 2, the library was moved from its temporary quarters in Dellwood Hall to the second floor of Tioga Hall.

The first floor of Tioga Hall, or "the basement" as it was so fondly referred, contained the Instructional Materials Center, the Audio Visual Center, the bookstore, the library office and book processing station, a photography dark room and the central power plant.

Tioga Hall – 1967

At the time the library was moved from Dellwood Hall to Tioga, the collection contained 26,000 volumes; 60 new oak study carrels were purchased for quiet study and daydreaming as students looked out over Empire Lake.

*Adding the top three floors on
Tioga Hall – 1967. Classes and
study went on as usual during
Tioga's expansion.*

The architect's design was unique. After the interior walls were built, the exterior walls (or "skins") of the upper levels, made from prefabricated reinforced concrete slabs, were lifted into place by a crane and secured at the corners.

All seemed to be in order during the Stage 2 construction of Tioga Hall; that is until the fall rains of 1967 arrived. As the story goes, the contractor was in the process of removing a portion of the six-inch slab of concrete that had been the temporary ceiling/roof of the library on the second floor in order to add the next three floors onto the building. Unfortunately, the contractor had not properly sealed or covered the construction zone above from the finished two floors below. It was the fall and rain was not predicted. On Labor Day of that year a heavy downpour occurred; water collected on the top of the building, filled the elevator shafts, and a "river" came cascading down the stairwell that led directly into the library and bookstore from the unfinished floors above. Water also seeped around the light fixtures in the library. President Brookins, with frantic prodding from the College librarian, was immediately on the phone with the contractor as the books and new carpets were getting wet. The disaster was mostly averted as the contractor hustled to spread tarps over the site and redirect the water, but as Besse Guthrie recalled: "When I came to work the next day, people said you had to be a spawning salmon to get upstairs. We had to wear boots and in one area of the library, I had to carry an umbrella! We had to set up these large fans that ran day and night in order to dry things out, but the library and bookstore continued to operate. We were very fortunate to have lost very few books."

While this art work by Phyllis Love was produced for the multi-image slide show at SWOCC several years later, and not as a drawing of the "almost disaster in the library," the artist without intention captured the image of how the water cascading down the stairs at Tioga Hall might have looked.

Stage 2 of the construction of Tioga Hall was completed in 1967. The third floor of the finished building housed the ASG offices, a new student lounge and a journalism office, as well as additional library storage space. The fourth floor housed the Study Center, the language classroom and laboratory, the Listening/Viewing Center, and faculty offices. The top floor was originally used as a temporary location for the art, homemaking, industrial drawing and blueprinting classes along with faculty offices. Bill Lemoine, forestry professor on campus, remarked that when he held his mapping class on the fifth floor of Tioga Hall, he was constantly hauling his students back away from the windows to pay attention to his lectures – the view in any direction was simply too enticing. The fifth floor would eventually house various administrative offices, including the president's office and the Board room.

Phase III of the Master Plan completed - 1968

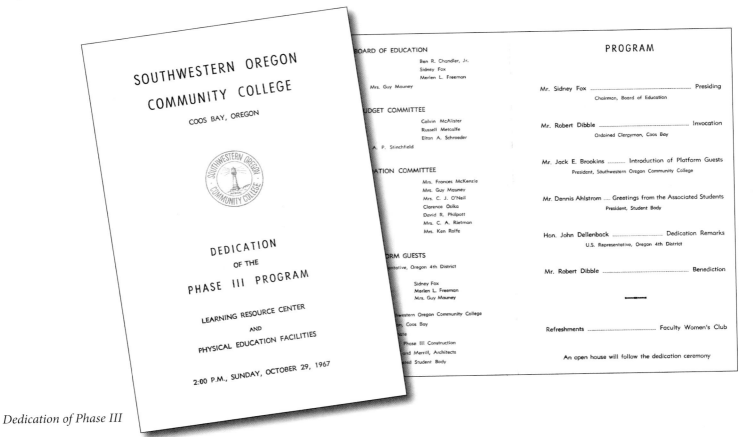

Dedication of Phase III

SOUTHWESTERN OREGON COMMUNITY COLLEGE

COOS BAY, OREGON

DEDICATION
OF THE
PHASE III PROGRAM

LEARNING RESOURCE CENTER
AND
PHYSICAL EDUCATION FACILITIES

2:00 P.M., SUNDAY, OCTOBER 29, 1967

BOARD OF EDUCATION
Ben R. Chandler, Jr.
Sidney Fox
Merlen L. Freeman
Mrs. Guy Mauney

BUDGET COMMITTEE
Calvin McAlister
Russell Metcalfe
Elton A. Schroeder
A. P. Stinchfield

ATION COMMITTEE
Mrs. Frances McKenzie
Mrs. Guy Mauney
Mrs. C. J. O'Neil
Clarence Osika
David R. Philpott
Mrs. C. A. Rietman
Mrs. Ken Rolfe

RM GUESTS
entative, Oregon 4th District

Sidney Fox
Merlen L. Freeman
Mrs. Guy Mauney

hwestern Oregon Community College
n, Coos Bay
ate
Phase III Construction
nd Merrill, Architects
ted Student Body

PROGRAM

Mr. Sidney Fox ———————— Presiding
Chairman, Board of Education

Mr. Robert Dibble ———————— Invocation
Ordained Clergyman, Coos Bay

Mr. Jack E. Brookins ——— Introduction of Platform Guests
President, Southwestern Oregon Community College

Mr. Dennis Ahlstrom —— Greetings from the Associated Students
President, Student Body

Hon. John Dellenback ———————— Dedication Remarks
U.S. Representative, Oregon 4th District

Mr. Robert Dibble ———————— Benediction

Refreshments ———————— Faculty Women's Club

An open house will follow the dedication ceremony

The construction of buildings and the infrastructure of the College facilities are only part of the success story at SWOCC. The staff worked hard to become recognized as a valid and viable school of higher learning by the State of Oregon. In 1967, the Northwest Association of Secondary and Higher Schools gave the College its first official certificate of accreditation. The entire campus got behind the effort, because certification not only meant they were recognized as a "real" institution of higher learning, but also the amount of State funding was directly related to the actual report itself. [10]

Undoubtedly, President Brookins went through several highs and lows when seeking additional financial support for expanding the campus. With the execution of the vision of the College in the hands of taxpayers, frustrating periods were normal. About the time of the water disaster in Tioga Hall, Brookins was to deliver a keynote speech at the Distinguished Award Banquet for the local chapter of the Jaycees in Coquille. Presumably Brookins had spent the day polishing his remarks to praise the Jaycees for their fine work in the community. However, just prior to the speech, Brookins got word that the Coquille School District #54 tax levy had been turned down by the voters – undoubtedly due to the softening economy discussed above. Therefore, on his way to the banquet, he revised his opening remarks as follows:

> *I'm going to give you some advice and you may not like it. I decided I'd give it to you straight when the voters spoke and said to children - money is more important than you are. The way to solve the problem is not to return to the fetal position; not curl up and go to sleep and hope that when you wake up things will be better.*

> *The State Legislature is half full of incompetent nincompoops! And the Senate is half full of incompetent old men! I know, because I've been there and watched them.* [6]

Turning our attention back to the funding of the College, in 1968 the citizens of the SWOCC district passed a new local tax base for the College in the amount of $750,000, the thought being that the new financial support level might eliminate the necessity of the College appealing to the voters for operating funds that were over and above the level provided by Oregon law – at least for a while. At the time, Oregon law provided that as long as a college budget stayed within a 6% increase from the prior year, the college did not have to obtain permission from the taxpayers to increase their budget by that amount. Using that formula, and given the original local property tax levy for the College back in 1961 of $362,649, the local property tax portion of the operating budget for the College in 1968 would have been $545,000 – an inadequate amount for the growing demands on campus. Hence the need for a new base to account for growth and inflation [22]

In the September 1971 special edition of *The World* newspaper, President Brookins was quoted as saying:

> *"Over four million dollars has been spent over the past eight years since the first bulldozer bit into the brush adjacent to Empire Lakes. In that time, 136,000 square feet of building space was created in seven buildings."*

Certification not only meant they were recognized as a "real" institution of higher learning, but also the amount of State funding was directly related to the actual report itself.

All colleges have what has been called the "Town-Gown" relationship – usually meant with a somewhat negative connotation either stemming from a budget/financing issue or the clash of generational differences. The evidence reviewed for this book does not support this concept between SWOCC and the towns surrounding the campus. In an effort to head off any of these types of issues, in the spring of 1968, the SWOCC Board established a College Community Council with six regional College-Community Liaison Committees scattered in the major towns within the district. The committee's objectives were fairly straightforward:

1. To improve communications between the College and the entire community;
2. To inform the communities about the programs offered on campus;
3. To improve communication with area schools;
4. To seek out the educational needs as expressed by the area citizens;
5. To assist the College in planning courses that meet the needs of the area citizens;
6. To assist the College in planning the infrastructure to meet the needs; and
7. To assist the College in interpreting the results of the information collected.

In the early '70s, the Faculty Senate also got into the act of expanding the opportunities for the community to experience the College. It was called the "Open Campus" concept. Essentially the process permitted anyone from within the College district to attend any class on campus they wanted for one week before actually enrolling and paying tuition and fees, the hope being that once a potential student experienced the quality of instruction for a chosen course, enrollment would increase and the College would build more goodwill within the community. It was a great idea, but it did not take root.

It's of note that in the late '60s a new organization was started on campus. It was called the "Golden Age Card Club." This was a club for seniors citizens over the age of 62; one could also qualify as a member if he or she were recently retired. The charter was very clear, "there are no dues and there are no meetings!" Once enrolled in the Club, members were eligible to participate in campus activities free of charge. Seniors could also enroll in classes at half price. By decade's end, the College had 273 seniors enrolled in the Club with 90 taking classes. The program grew and the name was changed to simply the Gold Card Club; however, the tuition benefit was suspended in the mid '90s due to necessary financial belt tightening at the College. Today, ALL students get a special tuition discount if they audit a course (not for credit). Gold Cards are still issued through SWOCC's Retired Senior Volunteer Program (RSVP) for individuals age 62 and above and provide free admittance to most area schools' events throughout the College district.

Ms. Helen Ferguson spoke to the issue of the age distribution of students in her interview with Mr. Vince Kohler back in 1978:

> "For the person who has not been around higher education and has not rubbed elbows with formal education for awhile, it is a very heady experience to sit in a class where three-fourths of the people are 10-20-30 years younger, and find that he or she can compete with those people. It is getting to be kind of a refrain that I hear repeatedly, especially at the beginning of Fall term, 'well, I've been out of school for 18 years and I'm scared to death to get in with a group of people who have just graduated from high school; I'm afraid I can't cope with them'. And to see that same person sit in there and not only cope with them but because of all the experience she/he picked up in running a family or a business or whatever kind of activity they've been in, they have background well beyond that of the 18 year olds. I like the intermingling of the young students with the older students. There is a rapport that's developed; it is a beautiful thing to see. It helps both of them to grow."

Phill Anderson remarked how much he liked the mix of students in his class during the late '60s:

> "There was a certain amount of liveliness that was caused by these differences. There were some students that may have been considered 'hippie types' by the locals, but to me who came from San Francisco, I looked at them as contemporaries of myself, because that is where I came from. I remember there being an older woman who drove every day from Powers and she would set some of these younger kids right on their ears as she described her real life experiences about how to survive in the logging camps of Oregon. The younger kids from Marshfield and North Bend who had never been out of Coos County in their entire life were infatuated with the stories from the students from San Francisco or Los Angeles. This action carried over into the student lounge where lively debates continued, and often included some of us younger professors."

Near the end of the decade, SWOCC students began capturing some of the better poetry, essays, line drawings, black and white photographs and short stories in a booklet they called *Spindrift*. Phill Anderson and Eric Muller were the initial faculty advisors until John Noland, the creative writing professor at the College, acquired the task – one he kept for almost 30 years. One such poem published in *Spindrift* is presented here as an example:

> i met the drifting play write this morning
> he gave me a speaking part in Monday
> but i wasted the day
> learning my lines
> > by Graham D. Wilson

In the early '80s, the editors of *Spindrift* changed the name to *The Beacon* which became the official literary magazine for the College. It was a student-run magazine which printed two editions per year. Originally, it was a supplement to the College newspaper, *The Southwester*. Each issue was presented in a public reading on campus and sold to interested parties. Entries were open to the public who submitted their original item in poetry, prose, photography, or graphics. In 1987, *The Beacon* placed second in the nation and two years later it received a first place award in the American Scholastic Press Association's yearly competition and did so in 13 of the next 15 years!

Follow us to The Beacon reading.

According to Professor Noland, as the reputation of *The Beacon* continued to grow, the College received material for publication from writers all over the nation, but only submissions received from within the College district were published – something to do with taxpayers funding the publication with "foreign" content. Nevertheless, his creative leadership and those of the students continued to acquire trophies for their work.

The first edition of *The Beacon* was published in 1968. When Professor Noland took over advising the editors of *The Beacon*, they instituted a blend of art and dance into the readings to make the material more appealing to a wider audience. For instance, dancers performed to readings of the student's poetry, students created and performed with life-sized puppets which class members made and wore as they mixed poetry with student-played music. With "tongue in cheek" Professor John Noland remarked in the February 3, 1990 edition of *The World*:

> *"One of the last things a graduate school advisor told me was to avoid becoming a college's literary magazine advisor, because that's the best place to get in trouble and get fired."* (45)

Obviously Professor Noland was very good at his job and never got fired! Presently, Dr. Candice Favilla serves as the advisor to the editors of the publication.

Another club formed by the editorial board of *The Southwester* in 1968 was called the Royal Order of Able Raccoons, or ROAR. The first recipient of the club's award – The Raccoon's Paw – was Tom Patch; the second Raccoon Paw recipient was Karl Gehlert, a member of the SWOCC Board of Education; followed by Lillian Sheryck, Edward Gray, Veneita Stender, Bill Lemoine, John Shilling, and Al Qualman. According to Stender, "It was student-sponsored and its purpose was to promote the College…getting publications out to the community."

At the end of the first decade of its existence, the SWOCC Master Plan on campus was about one-half done. It would be almost another ten years before Phase IV of the Plan would start. It was as if the administration paused to absorb what had been accomplished, embracing the assets that were created, and began to focus on building student programs rather than facilities.

As the community looked back over its shoulders at what had been accomplished at SWOCC over the past ten years, a true sense of pride had to have permeated their conversations. To think about the tenacity and grit it took to create reality from a dream had probably been forgotten by most, but a new college literally sprang forth from a swamp into a beautiful campus. The community was indeed proud. Enrollment at the College had grown from an initial student body of 256 FTE in 1961 to 1,227 ten years later. Even more remarkable is the fact that 48,700 people, young and old, attended classes during the decade and there was a strong connection between the industries, the communities and the local vocational jobs throughout the area. From providing classrooms and library space in ramshackle old facilities in the beginning to having modern building space at Empire Lakes was truly a remarkable feat.

SWOCC was on the move!

THE BUILDING YEARS

As SWOCC moved into the decade of the '70s, the Vietnam War was "front and center" in the minds of the young men on the SWOCC campus and throughout the nation. The draft lottery was implemented and student deferments were eliminated. Anti-war demonstrations remained highly visible on college campuses across the country. The daily toll of casualties in Vietnam was reported every night on the news – it was the first war in America where the daily horrors of war were delivered directly into our living rooms.

New terms would splash across the television screens as our vocabulary grew - OPEC, Watergate, rent control, gas quotas, M*A*S*H, mandatory busing, pet rocks, Prefontaine, double digit inflation, the Rubik's Cube, etc. Rising gas prices and long lines at local gas stations showed America just how vulnerable it was to foreign oil supplies. On the technology side, the VCR would change home entertainment forever. Star Wars created a whole new cult to rival Star Trek fans from the '60s. Politically, the outcome of the Roe vs. Wade case was finalized and there was a senseless slaughter at Kent State. A vice president (Spiro Agnew) and a president (Richard Nixon) of the United States resigned in disgrace under the threat of impeachment and America celebrated its 200th birthday. The minimum wage averaged around $2.50 per hour.

As was the case a decade earlier, the mainstream of SWOCC students was more interested in learning new skills and building their future plans than carrying signs, picketing or having peaceful sit-ins. The administration at the College continued to reach out to the community to provide the technical skills that the local industries wanted. About half way through the decade, the local economy saw a gradual erosion of its traditional resource based industries that blended well with the vocational programs offered on campus. The College was therefore faced with a rather politically complex problem. How should it develop new programs for retraining the growing number of displaced workers from the timber and fishing industries, provide educational opportunities for the returning veterans from Vietnam, provide general courses for the community at-large as well as continuing to provide freshman and sophomore transfer courses? Essentially, SWOCC was educating a group of people that would probably soon leave the community to find work in a profession that was jump-started by the classes taken at the College.

From a physical perspective, the campus remained isolated from the community. It was still difficult to see the buildings and landscape from Newmark Avenue and the campus politics generally remained contained behind a row of trees. One of the retired professors suggested that Brookins wanted to keep the row of trees as a visual barrier so that when people drove into the campus, they would get a real positive surprise. While President Jack Brookins was involved in community affairs, very few members of the faculty or administration were visibly involved off campus. Dr. Nathan Douthit, a well-known local author and distinguished history professor at the College, noted:

> "The College was enclosed on all sides by second-growth forests and underbrush. When you drove into campus, you left the developed residential and business districts of Coos Bay, North Bend and Empire out of view. Because the College was small, we got to know each other well as faculty members. Every month on pay day, we had a faculty happy hour, worked on committees and shared offices." [53]

There was a family feel to the College among all the departments. We would go off for a weekend at Camp Myrtlewood for fun and bonding.

As for the College community itself, professor Bower remarked on the family feeling on campus:

> *"The College was much smaller back then (1970s). There was a family feel to the College among all the departments. We would go off for a weekend at Camp Myrtlewood for fun and bonding. The finances were mostly tied to property taxes, tuition and the development of the workforce so there was a connection made to the community."*

Kirk Jones mentioned in an interview that he had only been on campus a couple of weeks when they had the Camp Myrtlewood retreat. After those couple of days, Jones felt he knew everyone from the custodian to the president. It was a remarkable experience. A similar comment was made by John Speasl who indicated that all were "expected" to mingle with others on campus!

Dr. Douthit summed up the composition of faculty during his tenure at SWOCC from 1969-1997:

> *"The faculty came with varied backgrounds of education and experience. They were a mix of former high school teachers, skilled tradesmen and teachers, retired military or second careers as teachers, business instructors right out of business careers and liberal arts teachers. Those who taught the transfer courses had to have at least a master's degree. Ben Fawver, Stan Elberson, Jack Swearingen, Hugh Hoyt, Ron Lilienthal, Chuck Hower and I all had doctoral degrees.*

> *"One of the healthy, if sometimes emotionally charged discussions between liberal arts and vocational instructors were over general education requirements for vocational students. Fortunately, because of the in-service and committee meetings involving representatives of both constituencies, there was general agreement on the need for reading, writing, and math standards and some limited exposure to the arts, social sciences and literature regardless of which program a student chose."*

During the '70s, the College continued to face the challenges presented by the economics of the region; high paying manufacturing jobs were disappearing rapidly and minimum wage service jobs were taken up by the younger generation. However, the tenets of the College remained the same: to provide quality classes for students wanting to transfer to a university at an affordable tuition rate; to provide for exceptional technical and vocational training courses for the industries in the region; and to provide adult education and guidance for retraining. Now another dynamic entered the equation – the returning veterans from the Vietnam War – some wanting to utilize the benefits of the GI Bill to gain employable skills, others simply taking the government's money as payment for their past service and wiling away their time in class.

1. Eric Muller	15. Gene Spencer	29. Terry Stahel	44. Don Stensland (back of head)
2. Chuck Hower	16. Bob Miller (cap & glasses)	30. Chris Rosman	45. John Rulifson
3. Dick White	17. Veneita Stender	31. Darrell Saxton	46. Jack Stevenson
4. John Noland	18. Hugh Hoyt	32. Tom Humphrey	47. Bev Kemper
5. Bob Dibble	19. Nancy Ruppe	33. Jack Anderson	48. Joe Babcock (cap & forehead)
6. Ron Stubbs	20. Jim Shumake	34. David Smith	49. Roger Barber
7. Barbara Brown	21. Jack Swearingen	35. Bill Krause	50. Don Burdg
8. Jack Brookins	22. Tommy Caranchini	36. Howard Hall	51. Phil Goetschalckx
9. Phill Anderson	23. Cheryl Robinson	37. Ron Lilienthal	52. Nelsine Burton
10. Bob Shepard	24. Kirk Jones	38. Vernon Sorenson	53. Barbara Dodrill
11. Carol Vernon	25. George McKenzie	39. Phil Ryan	54. Dori McArthur
12. Ben Fawver	26. Steve Ericksen	40. John Hunter	55. Connie Winger
13. Greg Pierce	27. Tom Wiedeman	41. Jim Love	56. Don Moffitt
14. Kathy Woolley	28. Beni Meacham	42. Nathan Douthit	57. Bill Sharp
		43. Bill Lemoine	

58. Carroll Auvil	65. John Speasl
59. Tony Burns	66. Joanne Cooper
60. Sam Cumpston	67. Bob Cooper
61. Helen Ferguson	68. Ann Hunt
62. Ed Chilla	69. Lanny Leslie
63. Barbara Jones	70. Andy Toribio
64. Dortha McCarthy	71. Harvey Crim
	72. Ray Kelley

The SWOCC crew at a retreat at Camp Myrtlewood – early 1970s.

Professor Bower described some of the population statistics when he first arrived in Coos Bay that helps to explain SWOCC's role in the community:

"When I came here in 1971 well over 50% of the adult population in the College district did not have a high school diploma. Further, I think about 60% of the high school graduates were not ready to start a college writing class and 70% or 80% were not ready for college level math. In response to this issue, SWOCC became one of the first colleges in the State to create a very robust Developmental Education Program to help bring the student's abilities up to entry level college standards. As well as a tutoring program tied to each department where the student's skills were deficient."

It would take several more years, perhaps 10 or more, before these programs got real traction.

The student profile on the SWOCC campus during the 1970-71 school year was as follows:

Full-Time Equivalent Students –	1,227
Vocational Students –	1,230
Lower Division Students –	832
Total Enrollment –	2,062
Average Age –	30.6 years
Men –	50.3%
Women –	49.7%
Married –	51%
Single –	49%

The forestry students at SWOCC planted trees on campus in commemoration of Earth Day.

The decade also opened with the nation's first Earth Day - April 22, 1970 - and SWOCC got involved. Aside from planting trees on the campus, outside speakers were brought to the campus to discuss environmental issues. Speakers such as Dr. Paul Rudy, Director of the University of Oregon Marine Biology Institute at Charleston, and Dr. Donald Watson provided students with important discussion topics on the environment. Shortly thereafter, the SWOCC Forestry Environmental Association was formed in an effort to open better communication between the campus and the community on environmental issues in the region. The April 30th edition of *The Southwester* that year carried an extensive article on the environmental teach-ins that were held around the campus on Earth Day. Lectures were offered by SWOCC professors Hugh Hoyt, Bob Dibble, Ben Fawver, Tom Loeber and Jim Shumake as well as additional speakers from around the community.

Later that year Ralph Nader, nationally renowned consumer rights advocate and environmental leader (and later a candidate for president of the United States for the Green Party), was brought to campus and presented a talk railing against the evils of corporate America. His talk spawned the impetus for students to form a chapter on campus of the Oregon Student Public Interest Research Group or OSPIRG.

OSPIRG could be considered an example of other environmental and consumer protection oriented organizations that sprang up across America to work similar issues. According to Holly Hall (Stamper), one of the founders of the OSPRIG chapter on campus in 1971, Peggy O'Neil, Peter Sorensen and other enthusiasts began circulating petitions among the SWOCC students and faculty which they planned to present to the College Board of Education to establish a chapter on campus. The petition read:

Publicity poster for Ralph Nader's visit to SWOCC.

> *We the undersigned students at SWOCC resolve that the OSPRIG shall be established. The purpose of OSPIRG shall be to articulate and pursue through the courts, the media, the institutions of government and other legal means, the concerns of students of the State of Oregon on issues of general public interest, in such areas as environmental preservation, consumer protection and corporate responsibility.*

> *OSPIRG shall be non-partisan, non-profit and student controlled. It shall be financed by an assessment of an added $1 per term per student. Any student who does not wish to participate shall be entitled to a refund at the end of each school year from the established public office.*

> *We hereby petition the SWOCC Board of Higher Education to authorize the establishment of OSPRIG.*

The Board of Education denied the petition, so the funding of the local chapter was mostly accomplished through voluntary dues and contributions. The organization simply drifted and was finally dissolved around 1973.

The College continued to offer outside speakers, not only on environmental issues but on a host of other topics. In fact, the College had a portion of the annual budget devoted to bringing nationally known people to campus every month for a lecture. Werner Von Braun, for instance, spoke to the students about space travel, and in the early '80s famous ocean explorer Jacques Cousteau's son Jean Michel was invited to campus to talk about Earth as a single system where everything was connected. This type of lecture series advanced the College in its relationship to the community. Even national political candidates visited the campus; probably the most famous were Robert Kennedy and Eugene McCarthy. Once the

Senator Robert F. Kennedy visited campus in June of 1968. (Stock photo)

Hales Center for the Performing Arts was completed in 2005 with a seating capacity of 501, the community had a first class auditorium in which to hear professional lectures and view performances with all the modern technology available.

Encouraged by the energy displayed on campus during Earth Day, an ad hoc committee raised the issue of smoking on campus. The goal of the committee was to eliminate smoking in the classroom, hallways and the campus at-large. They cited the conditions of cigarette butts littering the campus grounds, classrooms and halls, as well as damaging the carpets with burn holes, let alone the smoke pollution inside the classroom itself. In fact, the ventilation system in Tioga Hall would circulate the air from one floor to another and once the student lounge was located on the third floor, smoke from that floor would travel to the other floors above. Debates surrounding smoking - or rather not smoking - would remain a hot topic on campus for years to come. Today the SWOCC buildings are smoke-free, but the discussions to move to a tobacco-free campus are plentiful.

It seemed the College paused in the expansion of its physical footprint at the Empire Lakes site and turned its attention to enlarging the breadth of courses offered. It increased the number of courses and enlarged the faculty. While economic clouds were forming on the horizon, times were pretty good on campus.

New student lounge, third floor Tioga Hall – 1967 (note ash trays on tables).

In the early '70s, the forest products industry continued to dominate the employment picture throughout Oregon, and the local mills within the College district were in full production. The forestry technician program on campus had evolved into a professional curriculum where employers were very pleased to hire the graduates of the program. Bill Lemoine is credited with developing the growing program from being "vocational" to one being referred to as a "technical" curriculum – subtle, but an important distinction. As the number of students enrolling in the program grew, it was more than one instructor could handle. At one point there were over 50 students in the forestry program requiring three instructors, each holding a master's degree. Lemoine further commented that the forestry faculty at SWOCC had a personal mission for their students, "...our graduates will succeed and they will get jobs..." To provide additional teaching support, Bill Lansing, a forester from Menasha Corporation at the time, handled night classes for several terms.

During this time the forest technology program was being expanded at SWOCC, there were 13 other community colleges scattered throughout Oregon that were offering various levels of forestry technician programs. By the 1980s, the number of community colleges in Oregon offering forestry programs had dropped to nine, then slowly colleges one-by-one closed their programs; today there are only three community colleges offering the forestry curriculum – all in direct response to the shrinking demand for forestry technicians as the industry contracted across the west. Lemoine retired in December 1999 and the program was dropped from the catalog offering in 2003.

In the interview with professor Lemoine, he also touched upon transfer credits between SWOCC graduates moving on to Oregon State University to study forest management:

> *"In the beginning it was a very difficult situation, not just with SWOCC, but with all the community colleges that had a forestry program. It was a perpetual problem. We worked hard to get the transferability of courses accepted by the universities. They were the elitists and we were the stepchild!"*

When John Beuter became Dean at the OSU Forestry School in the mid '80s, these turf issues disappeared and graduates from the SWOCC program were accepted at the University with junior level status.

In 1970, the Forestry Club at SWOCC, under the guidance of Professor Lemoine, started the project to build a three-mile walking trail around Empire Lakes. The purpose of the trail was simple; it would provide students, faculty and the community at-large an opportunity to enjoy the beauty of the lakes, the campus and a natural forest setting. The forestry students gave up their weekends to hack out the walking trail and build five bridges that spanned bogs and portions of the lake. They used dead cedar saplings for pilings that were hand-driven into the mud with large sledgehammers. The last bridge to be constructed was built in the spring of 1973. It was over 150 feet in length and at one point crossed water that was 25 feet deep. Over open water, the bridge was supported by large floating logs donated by a local timber company.

The forest trail at SWOCC according to Professor Lemoine, 2010. Photo courtesy of Ward Robertson, 1978.

Over the years the marshy environment coupled with the areas rainfall required the Forestry Club to continually repair the trail. Over the past 40 years, students, faculty and community members have enjoyed the natural serenity of the trail provided by the now defunct Forestry Club.

For his work on campus during the decade Lemoine was granted entry into the Royal Order of Able Raccoons (ROAR), a rather mysterious club at SWOCC. Apparently the editor of the College newspaper at some point in time established the club and was the sole authority as to who got admitted. The author inquired of Lemoine if he recalled being selected, but he only had a vague recollection of what the organization stood for. The Royal Order faded away sometime in the 1980's

The SWOCC forest trail crossing a narrow/swampy ravine on Empire Lake.

The forestry students working on repairing the bridge using Dr. Fawver's duck boat that was kept in the boat house on campus.

with no record of its membership. The first nominee of the decade was Helen Ferguson.

Professor Lemoine remembered a special incident that occurred when a forestry conference was being held on campus. After a day of sitting in seminars, several of the visiting professors wanted to see what this forest trail was all about. Lemoine, being rightfully proud of the work done by his students, volunteered to lead the expedition. As described, there were several spots where the trail crossed portions of the lake or boggy areas where bridges were constructed. Since this conference was being held in the late summer, the lake was quite low and several of the bridges simply crossed dry ground.

As the group was walking across one of the bridges with Lemoine extolling the beautiful views around the Empire Lake, one of the visitors called his attention to something growing under the bridge, "Bill, it looks like there is a Marijuana plant growing under here." Professor Lemoine came back to take a look and quickly responded: "I'm a timber guy. I don't teach plant identification and furthermore I don't know anything about bushes and wouldn't know a Marijuana

The SWOCC campus trail through the forest is enjoyed by all!

Building bridges across Empire Lakes presented challenges for the forestry club. Note the large sledgehammer in the photo to the left. It was used to pound the cedar piling into the mud to support the bridge "timbers" - 1972.

plant if I saw one and my forestry students are innocent," which brought a real chuckle from his colleagues.

As the forestry program grew, SWOCC became well known across the western states as an excellent institution for training forest technicians. As a gesture of friendship on America's bicentennial, the College of the Redwoods in Humboldt County, California gave a redwood seedling to SWOCC. The forestry students on campus planted the tree three different times. Young redwood trees tend to grow relatively fast and each of the first two spots where it was planted simply could not accommodate the spreading limbs of the tree; today, its final spot is just outside the main entrance to Tioga Hall. It is now about 34 years old and over two feet in diameter.

Redwood tree, a gift from College of the Redwoods.

High climbing

Another method the College used to reach out to the community during the '70s was to provide a sporting event where all students could participate. It was called Skills Day and it drew high school and SWOCC students from within the College district to compete. In 1977, for instance, some 800 students competed in a total of 29 events. The day included feats of physical strength and coordination as well as competition in the classrooms in auto mechanics, welding, secretarial and accounting skills. The first place winners were granted a $50 tuition offset scholarship to attend SWOCC.

Log rolling

Engine dynamics

Log bucking

Log boom running

Welding

Choker setting

In the 1970s, distance learning at SWOCC got a real boost under the guidance of Bonnie Koreiva. Since the College district stretched for more than 50 miles from the Coos Bay campus in any direction, there was a need to provide advanced and vocational education to students who could not take classes on campus. Distance learning provided students with the opportunity to take college level courses off campus at a convenient time and location. Instructors from the College often conducted the classes. During the 1970s distance learning at SWOCC tripled! [42]

Class Year	Distance Learning Enrollment	No. Classes
1971-72	270	18
1972-73	691	46
1973-74	733	54
1974-75	1,574	105
1975-76	1,736	125
1976-77	2,216	145
1977-78	4,561	290
1978-79	6,246	n/a
1979-80	8,151	n/a

As "Distance Learning" has morphed into taking classes over the Internet, over 5,800 students have accessed e-learning opportunities from Southwestern since 2008.

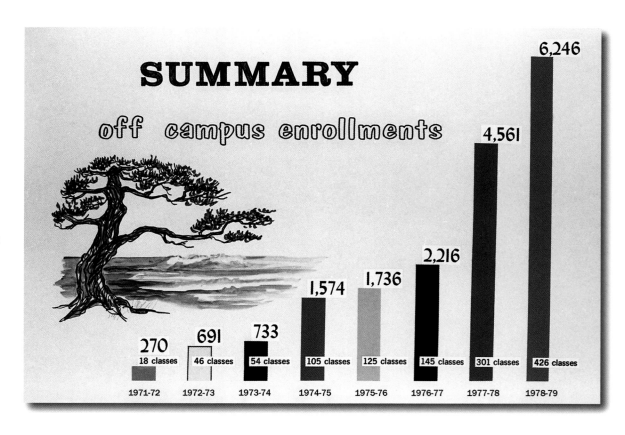

SUMMARY off campus enrollments

270	691	733	1,574	1,736	2,216	4,561	6,246
18 classes	46 classes	54 classes	105 classes	125 classes	145 classes	301 classes	426 classes
1971-72	1972-73	1973-74	1974-75	1975-76	1976-77	1977-78	1978-79

On April 1, 1975, the television channel 13 was started on campus. It took a tremendous effort on the part of the audio-visual department at the College, Warner Cable TV, students and members of the community to make the new station a reality. It was broadcast from the fourth floor of Tioga Hall from 8:00 a.m. to 8:00 p.m. with faculty members Dr. Terry Weaver as station manager and Ed Chilla as the executive director. While Weaver and Chilla were the only two faculty members involved in the production, 30 students from video class did most of the work. Channel 13 provided strictly non-commercial shows such as "Newsroom 13," a weekly roundup of community and SWOCC campus news; "Slim Trim," an exercise program; "Person to Person," an interview setting with JoAnn Cooper; "Story Time," where stories were read to small children by Eva Douthit; What's Going On; Man on the Street; Cable 13 News; Administrative News; and cooking demonstrations.

When no TV broadcasts were occurring, an FM radio station played in the background. In addition, five-minute air time was given to individuals in the community who wanted to express an opinion on some topic.

Channel 13 began on the SWOCC campus and was televised from the fourth floor of Tioga Hall. Pictured: Bonnie Koreiva, Ernestine and Don Moffitt - 1981.

For those who could not come to campus, during the winter term of 1975, the College offered four courses via the Oregon Public Broadcasting television network. The courses included Personal Finance and Money Management, Personal Health – Contemporary Health Issues, The New Literacy – An Introduction to Computers, and the Business of Management. Classes lasted for 30 minutes and were shown twice a week on cable systems. The classes could be audited (no tests – no grades) or for transfer credit. Another method of distance learning was born.

With the ever increasing application of technology, distance learning at SWOCC became available over the Internet with "online classes" beginning in about the year 2000. The program used the Learning Management System called WEBCT. Today the College uses a synchronized system called ANGEL (A New Global Environment for Learning) that allows students to view weekly lectures and assignments, take assessment tests, actively participate in online discussions through the "discussion board," and communicate with instructors, all in a virtual classroom setting – and on their own timetable. The programs continued to evolve, and since 2007 SWOCC has provided e-learning opportunities to more than 5,800 students scattered throughout the College district and beyond.

In order to broadcast the television signal, a large disc had to be placed on the top of Tioga Hall. The College hired the Menasha Corporation helicopter to lift the disc and position it atop the building.

While the records of the College do not reflect a lot of coursework involving the local Native American history, some classes were taught. In 1977, for instance, Esther Stutsman introduced a course entitled History of Local Indian Tribes – Part One.

The class was taught in the evenings at the Willow River Indian Benevolent Association Indian Museum in Empire. While having no formal training as a teacher, Ms. Stutsman presented topics on culture, customs, linguistic affiliations, social structure and oral literature. Stutsman was a member of the Coos Tribe and responsible for the Indian Museum; she was also a member of the local tribal council.

Esther Stutsman

Two years later, Adela Brubaker presented a course at the College on the beadwork of Native Americans. At the time, Brubaker worked at the Indian activity center in Empire. In 1978, Stephen Dow Beckham, a locally born historian, presented a week-long workshop at SWOCC on Indians of the Northwest Coast for public school teachers. The purpose of the workshop was to teach teachers how to use Beckham's book *The Indians of Western Oregon: This Land Was Theirs* in their classrooms. [78]

The fashion influence of the hippie movement in the '60s was again prevalent in the '70s. Veneita Stender, the associate professor of home economics during this period, described the late '60s and early '70s as a time when student attitudes about their image shifted. The conventional styles of dress and hair in the 1950s were replaced with the new "grungy/independent" look that demanded more creativity in teaching – not only in the making of clothing in her classroom, but for teaching in general.

As usual, life across America continued to evolve. Men sported shoulder length hair and non-traditional clothing became the rage, including bellbottom pants, hip huggers, colorful patches, hot pants, platform shoes, earth shoes, clogs, T-shirts, and gypsy dresses. The Beatles broke up and the death of Elvis Presley shocked the 1970s teenage generation.[16] The television comedy show "Happy Days" created a large following as it juxtaposed the differing cultures of its two main characters – Richie Cunningham and the Fonz (Arthur Fonzerelli). Even though SWOCC was mostly out of the mainstream movements prevalent on larger campuses across the country, a few of the fads did make it onto campus – "…men's hair was notably longer…" remarked Ms. Stender.

Some of the language of the 1970s: [32]

Get the skinny –	to get the facts
To psyche out –	to trick someone
Spaz –	clumsy
Dream on –	unrealistic
Far out –	really cool
Sick –	odd or unusual
You know –	a phrase to end a sentence
Chill out –	relax
Like –	a word to begin a sentence
Bear or Smokey –	police
Boob tube –	television
Dig –	to understand
Groovy –	cool, neat, awesome
Heavy –	intense
Pad –	home
Raunchy –	disgusting

Sports fans watched Lew Alcindor (a.k.a. Kareem Abdul-Jabbar) becomes the icon of the basketball court, while O.J. Simpson dashed for record yards on the gridiron. Johnny Bench, Reggie Jackson and Pete Rose lit up the diamond, while "Hammerin'" Hank Aaron blasted his 715th home run. Rose would later be convicted of illegal betting and removed from baseball forever. Mark Spitz won an unprecedented seven gold medals at the Olympic Games in Munich, Germany.

Speaking of sports, John Speasl (recently retired Athletic Director at SWOCC) has been an integral part of the athletic program at SWOCC from 1973 through the 50th anniversary year of the College – 2011. Asked how he came to the College back then, he said (with a twinkle in his eye):

"After the official interviews on campus, President Brookins took me to lunch. He ordered a gin and tonic and then asked me what I wanted. I didn't know how to react – was this a test or not, so I ordered a coke. A month later the College called and offered me a job as wrestling coach and instructor in health and physical education. At the time, I didn't realize that Jack was a real fan of athletics until after I was hired. I think he looked upon athletics as making the college experience at SWOCC a more complete program.

"Looking back, I can also credit him for making certain we had adequate funding for our athletic programs, at least during my first few years on campus. I also give a nod to the Longshoremen for giving their support to athletics at the College. They often showed up at Board meetings to insure that the core athletic programs of basketball (men and women), volleyball and track were not cut from the budgets."

Asked about his impression of the campus 38 years ago, Speasl went on to say that he felt very comfortable with the size of the College and the faculty welcomed him on board – a very common story from many who were interviewed for this book. He went on to say: "…however, in my area of athletics the campus felt a little crowded, we had to share lower Prosper Hall with many other disciplines. Drama had to share space with wrestling. After we had wrestling practice from 3:00 to 5:00 in the afternoon, we would roll the mats up and Ed Chilla would lay out his drama stuff from 5:00 to 7:00. The Student Union was on the third floor of Tioga and was quite small…"

Not only was there competition for space within Prosper Hall itself, the technology back then was pretty poor. There was only one telephone line that had to be used by all the coaches and staff on the mezzanine floor. Although each of the five coaches had their own phone, it meant that when the phone rang in Prosper Hall someone would pick it up then holler down the way to another coach who was wanted on the line so they could "pick up." Obviously, not the best impression left for a recruiting or marketing program.

Speasl went on to explain the rather intricate rules for recruiting high school athletes to the community college campuses spread across Oregon during the '70s. The Oregon Community College Association (OCCA) had determined that community colleges sprinkled along the I-5 corridor or located within the larger metro areas could not recruit high school athletes from "closed areas" – i.e., SWOCC, COCC, Blue Mountain, Clatsop districts were considered closed to athletic recruiting. However, community colleges that were in the closed group could recruit high school athletes from wherever they could find them. Notwithstanding these advantages, only 25% of the student athletes during the 1970s came from outside the SWOCC district, and most of these came from out-of-state.

The 1970s also saw the beginning of the technology revolution. After the arrival of the microprocessor, many different computer companies appeared and began developing their own microcomputers. Bill Gates and Paul Allen's Traf-O-Data company evolved into Microsoft. Steve Jobs and Steve Wozniak formed the Apple Computer Company. Compaq and Commodore were also new computer companies. These companies would change life as we knew it forever. [17]

As the computing hardware began to shrink in size and become more affordable, schools brought the Apple computer into their classrooms while businesses leaned toward the PC. A dichotomy began to grow as the language of the two competing systems was originally incompatible. IBM was left at the fringes. Technology growth in the '70s also saw the slow death of shorthand as secretaries and bosses learned to use dictation machines and typewriters with "memory."

The Data Processing Center at SWOCC in 1972 was an IBM 1130.

Back home in southwestern Oregon, computer technology had yet to penetrate, in any meaningful way, the forest products industries in the region. Truckload after truckload of one-log loads of old growth timber could still be seen passing through town on their way to a mill. The technology for sawing or peeling these big old logs was essentially done in the same manner it had been done for decades before. When the industry finally converted to high-tech late in the decade, the number of jobs it took to run a mill shrank by a factor of 10 – again displacing loyal long-term employees who did not have the computer skills to adapt.

However, people along the coast still looked to the natural resource industries for work. If a person had a union job at one of the big mills during the decade they were pretty well set and their job was secure – at least for a few more years. Wages were strong and the demand for new houses throughout America was running at record levels. That being said, it was difficult for a young person just out of high school to find a job locally as many of the forest product companies were not expanding and the technology boom was still stranded in Silicon Valley. Therefore, high school graduates looked to SWOCC to advance their skills. Even after completing a degree program at SWOCC, many young people left the area in search of fortunes elsewhere as there were limited jobs locally. From the window of hindsight, it is apparent that the decade of the '70s would be the nexus of the forest products industry after dominating the economy of Oregon for over a century.

Asked to explain how the campus life changed over the first 20 years of existence, the comments of Professors Bower, Anderson and Dodrill summarize as follows:

> *"The campus life changed as the students and instructional mission evolved. In the early '70s the veterans returning from the Vietnam War showed up with a greater maturity than the traditional student and had a greater depth of experiences to share. (In general, the student population on campuses across the nation, as well at SWOCC, became a bit older and mature. They wanted to get involved in student government.) The students seemed less distracted from their studies. Some returning GIs were not interested in doing college work and simply came to class when they wanted and used their GI funds for other purposes.*
>
> *"As the mills began closing in the late '70s, the College offered more assistance and retraining programs to the displaced workers. Greater funding became available through state and federal grants to help retrain the workers who lost their jobs in the timber and fishing industries."*

Pete Sorensen, a SWOCC student from 1970-71, explained it this way:

> *"I attended class with people that were five years older than me who had just returned from the War and another student who was 75 years old who had never gone to college. He was like my grandpa! I also had housewives who were returning to college. Another factor tossed into the mix was the contact between the traditional academic freshman and the conservative-practical person pursuing a two-year degree in a vocational field. That mixture provides an education in and of itself, because you are talking with people that have a completely different life history than I did."*

The record at SWOCC clearly demonstrates the fact that the administration was in tune with what was going on in the community. Vocational retraining increased in the '70s, but not at the loss of the teaching of transfer level courses. In fact, many of the programs that might have been called vocational a decade earlier were now two-year technical programs taught by an instructor with a master's degree. The College could then present graduates with an Associate of Arts degree that would allow the recipients to transfer to a four-year institution and continue their education at the junior level. On the other hand, the AA degree demonstrated to would-be employers that the student had received a broad education and was therefore potentially capable of a wider range of responsibility. Programs were still being offered on campus to help an apprentice move toward a journeyman classification, but these were on the decline.

Mushroom Identification class.

However, some of the classes were still held just for fun.

During the '70s a new class was offered by the College that had nothing to do with finding a job. It simply involved teaching nature lovers which mushrooms were good to eat and which ones would kill you! Joanne Wright took students on walks through the woods looking for mushrooms with unlikely names such as Chicken of the Woods, Inky caps, Boletus, Shiitake, Chanterelle and Cauliflower mushrooms, etc. Of course, Ms. Wright always was sure to point out the ones that were deadly poisonous like the Gem of The Woods and other species of Amanita. The mushroom class generally celebrated their expedition with a cook-out on campus where Joanne's students cooked up several varieties of mushrooms. Undoubtedly, the teacher was the one who "took the final exam" by tasting each dish and passing judgment. The presumption is that there were no serious consequences from the final exam as the class was offered for many more years.

In an interview with *The World* newspaper back in the late '70s, Wright listed the most common questions asked of her:

Q. *How can you tell if a mushroom is edible or not?*

A. *You can't unless you know what mushroom you have!*

Q. *Are there any tests to tell an edible mushroom from a poisonous one?*

A. *No! All tests are unreliable!*

Q. *Will cooking make poisonous mushrooms edible and safe to eat?*

A. *No! 98% of the time cooking does not remove the toxin.*

Q. *Can mushrooms be eaten raw?*

A. *Yes! But don't eat the poisonous ones.*

Q. *Do poisonous mushrooms grow beside the good edible ones?*

A. *Yes!*

Q. *Are poisonous mushrooms called toad stools?*

A. *The word toad stool is simply a slang word for mushroom. It is best not to use that term at all.*

In the interview with Ms. Holly Hall (Stamper) in 1971, she indicated that one of the most positive things she recalled about SWOCC was the fact that you had direct access to the instructor who actually taught the class; unlike at the university where you might get access to a T.A. (Teaching Assistant) who was working on an advanced degree and was a student himself (or herself). Ms. Stamper may have been one of the first high school students in the State that was allowed to enroll in a community college while still attending high school and younger than the requisite 18 years of age; again demonstrating the diversity of the student body and the challenge for the instructor to strike the right balance.

Dr. Patty Scott, the current president at SWOCC, touched on this very topic when interviewed about her two years as a student at Lane Community College in Eugene:

> *"What strikes me about my time at Lane was how it framed my desires about making a career out of working at the community college level. I had worked at a private university back east, the University of Oregon and other community colleges, so I had a good perspective how each functioned. At Lane (and now at SWOCC) they really listened to the student with the goal of trying to help them by really getting to know them individually. I learned that I really liked helping students determine their individual course of study."*

The mixture of the students could have caused some real problems in managing the classroom setting. One group of students in class might have been composed of dislocated older men who had lost their job as loggers; others might be divorced women who were struggling to raise a family and hold down a job at the same time; a Vietnam veteran who really did not care to be in class; and a grandmother who simply was interested in the subject. Into the mix came high school graduates, some ill-prepared for college life, as well as regular college students who were on a transfer course to the University of Oregon and were only at SWOCC for financial reasons.

Phill Anderson commented on teaching an English class composed of just such a mixture:

> *"I loved it. The trick was to play the class like an orchestra. Every student's opinions are important and letting their creativity come out made the learning experience rewarding – even if a few egos were bruised in the process."*

His teaching method must have mirrored a referee in a wrestling match!

Ms. Stamper went on to talk about SWOCC being a commuter college, which mirrored the comments made a decade earlier by Professor Croft. There was no on-campus housing, no student buses, and - contrary to the original Master Plan - no football team around which the students could rally. In response to an interview question as to why the College never developed a football team, Dr. Steve Kridelbaugh, SWOCC president from 1990 to 2005, indicated that it cost about $1,300 to outfit one football player and in his judgment football was a money losing proposition for the College.

As mentioned, the economies in Coos, Curry and Douglas counties were showing considerable cracks in the forest products and fishing industries that had been the mainstay in the area for the past 100 years. A story relayed in an interview of Mr. Jeff Manley, manager of Community Action Center, back in 1984 offers some levity to finding a job in Coos Bay during the '70s: [22]

> *"When I came here in 1973, a man from Arkansas came to see me in my office. He was an older man. He said: 'I came here to work. I understood there was a lot of opportunity, but I can't find a job. I've spent all my money getting out here and I am mad. I want you to help me find a job.' I said that I had no idea if he wanted to work in the woods or in the mills at his age. Where do you think you are going to work, I asked?*
>
> *"He said, 'You know, the South is plastered with brochures, pamphlets and leaflets, saying Come to Coos Bay, Come to Coos Bay to work.' So I asked, do you have one of those pamphlets for me to see? He said he had one in his truck and went to retrieve it. When he returned, he was carrying a small pamphlet and it did say Come to Coos Bay, but it was dated 1946, and he had waited until 1974 to make the trip."*

There was an important political issue that surfaced in the 1970s that involved land use planning and the growth of the area. Early in the decade, Governor Tom McCall and the Oregon Legislature had established ironclad rules around all land development in Oregon when Senate Bill 100 was passed and signed into law. No acre of land in the State would escape the regulations that were put into effect. This much-debated bill created the Land Conservation and Development Commission in1973. The LCDC placed every county and incorporated town into a system of statewide land use planning goals and guidelines. Hearings drew thousands of participants to meetings – some turning into outright brawls as the pioneer spirit of Oregonians resisted governments telling them how to use their private property. As SWOCC expanded, it too would have to buckle under to the State's planning guidelines, but it also gave the College leverage over the type of future land uses that surrounded the boundary of the campus.

In the tradition of "bucking the tide," President Brookins continued to push forward with the expansion of the campus infrastructure until his retirement in 1985. In fact, Presidents Brookins and Kridelbaugh can be credited with building all of the major buildings that comprise the current Coos Bay college campus. Dr. Kridelbaugh started the process of establishing a complete satellite campus in Curry County and President Scott made it a reality.

In 1978, work began on planning for a College Community Center on campus, or as it became known, Empire Hall, at the south end of Empire Lake. Land use and environmental regulations required that the building be set back from its original position an additional 30 feet from the lake. This required the cost estimates to go over budget, so the bookstore that was planned as part of Empire Hall had to be scrapped. The construction of Empire Hall was undertaken by the firm of Baughman and Associates for a cost of $1,112,400. The completion, celebration and dedication would not occur until 1980.

Mr. Phil Giuntoli, the architect in charge of the design, explained the concept behind the building:

> "It (The College Community Center) is a wooden triangle floating on a cement pad by the shores of Empire Lake. It is a response to what students, faculty and others feel about existing spaces on campus and what they wanted to see in a building designed specifically as a community center. It stretches two stories, holds a slim 16,000 square feet of space in a manner that makes it look larger than it really is." [44]

Artist rendition of Empire Hall ca. 1977.

Empire Hall rises from the mud – 1978

Empire Hall under construction -1978. Photo courtesy of Ward Robertson.

Shown here are the upper and lower entrances to Empire Hall and the Hales Center for the Performing Arts. Twenty years after Empire Hall was completed, the Center was added.

Empire Hall looks out on the serene setting of Empire Lake. As the story is told in the December 21, 1981 edition of The Southwester, Empire Hall lost a third of its front glass wall in the 100 M.P.H. winds of Friday the 13th (December). The loss was covered by insurance. The downed trees scattered around campus were cut into firewood by members of the forestry and fishing technology clubs.

Senator Mark Hatfield – 1980.

On March 29, 1980, Senator Mark Hatfield was on hand to help dedicate Empire Hall; over 400 people from the community attended the celebration and heard the Senator's remarks:

"I was on hand sixteen years ago to dedicate the first two original buildings on the Empire Lakes campus. The community colleges have been out front recognizing the need for practical education in preparation for entering the labor market. There is a perception that the universities have lost much of the will to teach for teaching's sake. Community colleges offer viable alternatives to post-secondary education and offer healthy challenges to the university mystique. They can redeem higher education from falling prey to the entrapments of over extended research and publishing by providing solid practical education."

Hatfield went on to say that students who have achieved success at the two-year institutions will be looking for advanced education and provide a ready pool of new undergraduates and graduate-level students at the universities.

It could be said that the first two decades of the College were the formative years at SWOCC – getting the district formed, a tax base established, employees hired, property acquired, a union formed, and several buildings constructed; all with the support of the local community.

But let's not forget the student. Asked to describe the typical student who attended SWOCC during the first two decades, no one interviewed for this book could really come up with a "one liner." That is because the groups that came to the campus were from very different backgrounds. Some were just out of high school and wanted an inexpensive way to complete their first two years of college before transferring; some were just out of high school and wanted a partial or degree-based vocational program. Others were just taking classes out of interest or need for retraining. Students ranged in age from eighteen to eighty something. It is no wonder there was no definition of the "typical student."

One of the highlights of the 1978 graduation ceremony at SWOCC was the presentation of an honorary college degree to Henry Hansen. At the reception following the ceremony, someone asked Henry, "So you're the man we have to thank for having a college?" Henry responded modestly, "Maybe someone else could have done it bigger and better." Bigger maybe, but certainly not better!

Henry Hansen received an honorary college degree from SWOCC in 1978. Pictured: Bob Croft, Henry Hansen and Helen Ferguson.

THE FINE TUNING YEARS

Following the completion of Empire Hall, it took President Brookins only three years to add five more buildings to the campus; Eden Hall, Sunset Hall, Sumner Hall, Fairview Hall and Lampa Hall were built along with a fire training tower. With the completion of these buildings, the College would shift its focus in the 1980s from construction of buildings to development of programs and courses to help the community transition from a resource based industry.

Construction of Eden Hall, Sunset Hall and Sumner Hall – 1981-82.

Aerial view of the SWOCC campus in early 1981. Eden Hall is a 104-seat auditorium, fully multi-media equipped for presentations and lectures. Photo courtesy of Ward Robertson.

In late 1979, work began on the construction of a fire training tower. The forestry class on campus got an opportunity to participate in clearing a portion of the three-acre site using old-fashioned logging techniques such as the two-man falling saw affectionately known as a "misery whip." The students also got experience using a modern chainsaw. While less modern techniques were used to clear away the trees, modern building techniques were used to erect the fire training tower.

Fire tower construction.

The fire tower and mockups of vehicles and boats were used as part of a two-year Associate of Science degree in Fire Science. It gave students and other firefighters in town "real life" drills that are faced in a building fire. For instance, during a smoke drill, students have to pack all their equipment and tools, including a breathing apparatus, to the top floor of the tower, through "a maze of walls and doors," while learning to keep a cool head, stay low and breathe slowly. An additional benefit flowed to the community as a result of having the fire training facility. Apparently, insurance costs were much lower for a community that had a fire training facility than for a similar city without one.

About the time the fire tower was being built, the softball field was under construction. It was a community project requested by the local softball association. In the end, it got included in the capital campaign to build Eden, Sunset, Sumner, Fairview and Lampa Halls. The local longshoremen's union signed on to help insure the passage of the vote, as one of their members (Don Banta) was an avid baseball player.

Early in 1980, Bob Hudson, a local realtor in Coos Bay and retired president of the All Coast Fisherman's Association, suggested the College develop a vocational training program for the deckhands who worked on the fishing vessels out of the Charleston harbor. Supporting the proposal was the fact that there were 4,400 commercial fishing vessels working the ocean fisheries in the State of Oregon, 1,762 of which were harbored along the South Coast. Each vessel employed anywhere from one to four people in addition to the captain. Turnover of deckhands ranged from 20% to 25% each year, and the cost and risks associated with "OJT" added to the rising cost of an already marginal business. SWOCC established a training program that year and 35 students applied, but only 24 qualified for entry into the program. In total, the course required three terms to complete the training, which included fish net mending, vessel and product hygiene, navigation, basic seamanship, first aid, cooking at sea and firefighting. Seventeen captains from the Charleston harbor volunteered their boats as working laboratories, and a $240,000 grant funded the program and paid the students minimum wages while they were taking the courses.

The marketing campaign for the Fisheries Technology program at SWOCC – 1981.

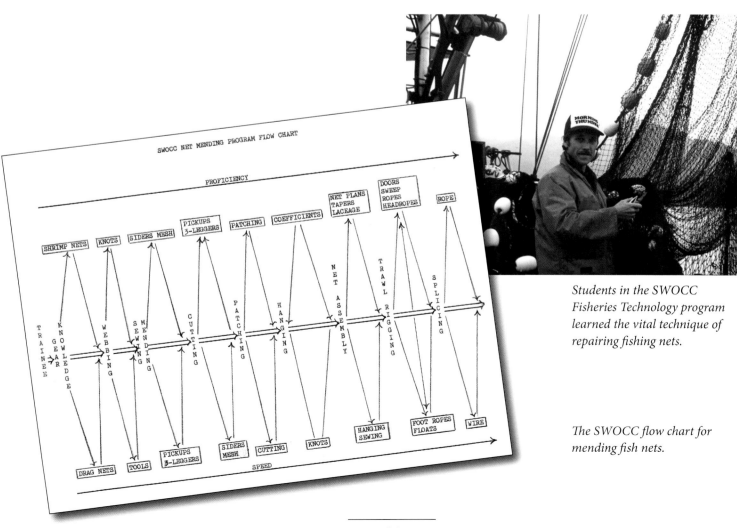

Students in the SWOCC Fisheries Technology program learned the vital technique of repairing fishing nets.

The SWOCC flow chart for mending fish nets.

While technical skills were taught in the program, safety was emphasized at every opportunity. Knowing what to do on board a vessel in case of an emergency and knowing how to stay alive when something goes wrong were essential elements of the course. According to Nick Furman, the course instructor, "One of the reasons the College started teaching the class was because we saw a lot of sloppy seamanship and poor navigation and those things have resulted in some tragic circumstances at sea." For instance, Furman held a survival suit workshop at Empire Lakes to show how to put them on in both dry and wet conditions. [65]

A year or two later and under the auspice of Workforce 2000 Skills Center at SWOCC, a portable math kit was developed for men and women who were working and could not attend classes in person. According to Veneita Stender:

A maritime worker in Charleston, Oregon examines a portable math kit that was used in the rural workplace literacy project at Southwestern Oregon Community College.

"One of the goals of the program was to reduce the barriers for bringing education to the people who were working a day job by taking the classroom to them. The pilot project was designed to test the delivery system by using math materials in portable kits as a proxy." [46]

One of the targets of the pilot program was the men and women working on the fishing vessels moored in Coos Bay. A financial grant to support the program came from the American Association of Community and Junior Colleges. SWOCC was one of only ten colleges across the nation to qualify for the grant.

On the national front, one might describe the decade of the 1980s as the "me decade" as the older baby boomers (born between 1946 and 1964) began to hit their stride and climb the corporate and academic ladders. A study by UCLA and the American Council on Education indicated that incoming college freshmen during the decade were more interested in status, power, and money than at any time during the past 15 years. Hence business management courses were more popular than ever, as were advanced degrees for those destined to work at the college level.

The '80s were also characterized by Mount St. Helens, Princess Di, the women's movement, Cabbage Patch Dolls, the Game Boy and Pac-Man; Cheers and Rosanne attracted a certain following on television; Ronald Reagan pushed his theory of supply-side economics and the credit card revolution gained traction; Tootsie, E.T. and The Terminator reached the silver screen; and the Challenger explosion sent shudders throughout America and set the U.S. space program back a few years. John Lennon's death saddened America; on October 19, 1987 the stock market collapsed on Black Monday; the AIDS virus was identified; Michael Jackson introduced the moon walk to a youth culture captivated by MTV; the compact disc (CD) helped launch the Blockbuster movie rental business; the Exxon Valdez, the "Super Mom", and the dismantling of the Berlin Wall were all a part of the '80s fabric. The average minimum wage during the decade was $3.10 per hour and the decade started in a very deep national recession.

Efforts to censor books tripled in the '80s. For instance, *The Adventures of Huckleberry Finn*, *The Grapes of Wrath*, and *Catcher in the Rye* were among books banned in New York State school libraries. Roget's Thesaurus banned sexist categories: mankind became humankind; countryman became country dweller. Columbia University, the last all-male Ivy League school to go co-ed, began accepting women in 1983. President Reagan endorsed a constitutional amendment to permit school prayer. It was defeated. [17]

The boomer generation continued to grow in its influence on the American landscape. They were well educated, aggressive and armed with strong computer skills. Many joined the ranks of academia and as one philosopher indicated, they brought along with them the freedom of thought and expression prevalent in the 1960s. More single family households were being created by a too-easily married and too-easily divorced national culture. President George H. W. Bush called for a kinder and gentler nation with no new taxes. And there developed a communication gap between the technology generation and the know-how generation that occupied the top rungs of corporate America and the senior professor positions in academia.

Fashion and entertainment took another turn during the '80s. The combination of Nancy Reagan's elegance and Princess Di's love of fashion stimulated a return to opulent clothing styles across the nation. Teens not wearing designer clothes opted for Michael Jackson's glove or Madonna's fishnet stockings, leather, and chains. Older women wore the Out of Africa look popularized by Meryl Streep. The fashions seen on the SWOCC campus were similarly mixed. Ms. Stender remarked that there was a huge influx of women into her clothing construction class during the '80s, and they moved to the upper floor of Tioga Hall in order to accommodate the need for a larger classroom. Image won over reality and tanning salons thrived, despite warnings by dermatologists nationwide. Cable TV was born during the decade and over 60% of American households with a television received it through cable networks.

The language of the 1980s: [33]

Ace –	the best
Airhead –	stupid
Bad –	really good
Bookin –	to get away from a location very quickly
Choice –	extremely cool
D.I.N.K. –	Double Income No Kids
Dis –	disrespectful
Freddy –	a beer
I kid you not –	I am telling the truth
Kickass –	awesome or excellent
Lame –	not cool
Roller –	police
Sick –	cool
Space cadet –	someone who does not know what is going on
'Sup –	what is going on – what's up?
To veg out –	hang out on the couch and rest a lot

Sports fans watched Julius Irving perform his "magic" on the basketball court along with the likes of Larry Bird, and a young graduate from the University of North Carolina by the name of Michael Jordan would launch a spectacular sports career. Roger Clemens would strike out 20 players in one baseball game. Joe Montana and Jerry Rice would team up to dominate the game of football.

In 1984, the residents of Oregon approved a lottery system to help stimulate the economy and help the State out of the doldrums of a recession. The lottery grew rapidly in popularity as new games and promotions increased player options. Gambling profits from the lottery proved irresistible to legislators who appropriated them to meet the costs of basic social services. It would not be until 1995 that Oregon voters directed a portion of annual lottery proceeds to be used to finance public education.

Later in the decade, William G. Robbins, historian from Oregon State University, documented the precipitous decline in the Coos Bay economy in his book *Hard Times in Paradise*:

> *"Then came the whirlwind—a rash of layoffs and mill closures in 1979 led by the Georgia-Pacific Corporation's plywood operation, one of the largest employers on Coos Bay. What followed in the next few years was a hemorrhaging of well-paid industrial jobs as one mill closure followed another. Coos Bay gained a new reputation as the State's most depressed area.*

> *"Coos Bay communities were pacesetters for mill closures everywhere across the Northwest during the 1980s. Even when a few mills reopened, they did so with new automated equipment and sharply reduced workforces. A stagnant forest-products market, mechanization, and sharply diminished timber stands continued to erode Coos Bay's industrial base. Except for retirement settlements, the South Coast economy has continued to languish through economic hard times."*

One might also note that the fish stock in the ocean that once supported a major fishing industry in Coos County had significantly declined. The federal government stepped in under the jurisdiction of the Endangered Species Act, as well as the Magnuson Fishery Conservation and Management Act, and began limiting the quota and type of species – especially the native silver or Coho salmon – that could be caught. The fishing fleet and the fishing families whose lives depended upon a predictable quota dwindled. It hit the commercial fishing fleet hard all along the Oregon, Washington and California coasts. Many sold their boats and simply left the area, while others sought retraining and new skills at the SWOCC campus.

As the '80s were unfolding, the recession that started in late 1979 was beginning to abate throughout the nation by mid-decade. However, the recovery would bypass the coast of Oregon. In December 1984, for instance, three of the four counties with the highest unemployment percentages in Oregon were contained in the SWOCC district boundaries - Curry, 19.3%; Coos, 15.7%; Baker, 14.2%; and Douglas, 13.7%. State employment figures revealed relatively low percentages of unemployment in the State's four major metropolitan areas — Eugene-

Springfield, Medford, Portland, and Salem, but the timber and fishing dependent towns within the College district were still reeling from the impact of the recession. It seemed that the sign "COOS BAY - The World's Largest Lumber Shipping Port" still stood, though somewhat battered and looking unsteady. By the early '80s it was obvious that it had outlived its message. For many, the College stood as a way to weather the times. "Family-wage-jobs" continued to migrate out of the coastal counties as mill jobs dried up. The classic urban vs. rural political controversies became much more prevalent and the funding of schools, at all grade levels, was at the forefront.

Athletic programs at the College were the subject of heated debates at budget meetings throughout the decade as the College grappled with funding issues. During the late '70s, wrestling, cross country and tennis had been added to the intercollegiate programs. They were cut for two years from 1982 to 1983 with tennis never returning. Basketball, track and volleyball were always funded. Funding for the wrestling and cross country teams had to be obtained from outside sources. The decade started out with four coaches and ended with three. (See Appendix)

Recruiting high school athletes to the College also changed. As mentioned earlier, not only did the recession of the early '80s impact the communities at-large, it also had a negative impact on enrollment in the high schools within the College district. During the 1960s and '70s, Marshfield High School was one of the largest schools in the State and consequently was fertile ground for athletic recruitment for SWOCC. This changed dramatically as the recession took hold.

In 1983, SWOCC joined the Northwest Athletic Association of Community Colleges (NWAACC) along with merging with the Washington community colleges for tournament play. Merging with the Washington colleges for tournament play reduced the expenses of sending teams to national tournaments – often clear across the country. The only caveat was that members of the college wrestling team that were good enough were allowed to go to the National Junior College Athletic Association tournaments.

The NWAACC was established to provide simpler access to high school coaches for recruiting athletes (and offering them scholarships) from Washington, Oregon, California, Nevada and Idaho – with Montana joining in 1992 and Hawaii in 2008. Also, SWOCC got modern by giving all the coaches on campus their own telephone lines! By the end of the decade, 50% of the athletes attending SWOCC were from outside the College district.

While recruiting athletes from outside the district helped with the FTE funding, it appeared that the administration of the College did not see the value generated by the athletic program. In 1986, then college president, Bob Barber proposed dropping all athletics at SWOCC and using the savings to fund the Displaced Homemakers program. A special Board meeting was held after numerous on-campus and community meetings were held to discuss the proposal of dropping athletics altogether; a ballot was delivered showing that only five faculty members on campus agreed with dropping sports from the curriculum. The majority were opposed to losing athletics, so the Board approved funding the

The community in general trusted the College and saw it as a resource for their future. The faculty and the students were focused on learning to get a job and move on.

basketball programs for men and women, track and volleyball. One might say that during the latter part of the decade, athletics at SWOCC was "under siege."

One of the students who availed himself of the benefits of the G.I. Bill was Mark Hamlin. He not only graduated from SWOCC, he went on to become a member of the College's Board of Education. As a Board member he recalled a story that is worth repeating here:

> *"One issue I recall was the need for an elevator in Prosper Hall. A number of students were disabled, and the Disabled Veterans of America (DVA) were vocal about the need for an alternative to physically carrying a wheelchair bound individual up the steps for graduation ceremonies or other events. As a Board member-elect I had addressed the issue to President Brookins and Board members to no avail. Soon after being elected to the Board and during a Board of Education campus tour we came to the steps of Prosper Hall where members of the DVA and a camera crew from KCBY (local television station) were coincidentally present. A suggestion was made as to which Board members would volunteer to carry a wheelchair bound veteran up the steps. The event put the elevator on a fast track."*

With the migration of families out of the College district, the increase in single parent households, and the enrollment of the more capable high school graduates directly into four-year institutions, SWOCC saw a marked decline in the readiness of its entry level freshmen to do college level work; this even as the yearly increase in enrollment continued to set record levels. A statistic in 1990 reveals a growing challenge facing the College. Of the total enrollment at SWOCC in 1990 of 9,528 students, 1,473 were classified as "program students" – i.e., they had declared their major during registration; fully 1,131(77%) of those were classified as academically disadvantaged – i.e., not prepared for college level work – per their placement tests. Over 60% of all entering freshmen at SWOCC scored below college level on the English reading and writing placement test, and 70% scored below college level on the mathematics placement test. Clearly the College was facing a new challenge.

Into this arena stepped Dr. Robert "Bob" Barber, who was selected as the third president of the College in 1985. According to a 1986 article in *The World*, Dr. Barber reported that "…his first year was spent sweeping out the halls of academia – shifting staff, negotiating retirements, setting new rules of the day – and now predicts a year of introspection at the College. No more crisis management. Barber spent his first year cutting the budget, trimming personnel, reorganizing the administration, and pushing forward work on a mission and goals statement…" The article went on to capture some of Barber's focus on the youth of the district: "I went to speak to the eighth grade graduates of the Reedsport School District. I think it's important to reach this group, because they can still be influenced and because their parents are there listening with them. I told them to look to their left and their right…one of the three will not finish high school. Another of you three will not go on to advanced training. Their parents know, from neighbors who have lost jobs, what happens to those two. We hope SWOCC will provide them with an answer to what can happen to their own student…" [68]

In a later interview for this book, Barber further described his experience when taking over the leadership role at the College:

"When we arrived in 1985, the general community morale and the morale at the College were very low. Yet there was a core group of leaders in both the region and at the College who held a vision that the area would survive and remake itself. The community in general trusted the College and saw it as a resource for their future. The faculty and the students were focused on learning to get a job and move on, often out of the community or to a university. There was little student activism with more interest on financially surviving and getting through. The level of educational skills needed for entry level students at SWOCC changed rapidly during the 1980s and students who formerly could find work without basic skills found themselves without work and unprepared to go on to college or return to college.

"My greatest challenge was to bring in new ideas and innovative ways to manage the College more effectively, reduce costs and introduce new types of programming. The College was not accustomed to the shared governance model of leadership I introduced and some individuals had some reservations about sharing information openly across the campus."

Another issue facing the College was the number of people within the district who had their high school years interrupted and later realized that a high school diploma was a valuable commodity in the job market. Kathy Walsh was put in charge of the program that provided an opportunity for these people to obtain a General Education Diploma (GED). In the first year of the program, she had planned for about 20 students to enroll, but 40-50 students signed up in each of the first three terms, indicative of the local economy and a hope that a better education would open up new options for out-of-work men and women.

The clippings from local newspapers on file at the College are filled with testimonials of those who obtained their GEDs from SWOCC. A recent enrollee in the GED program had this to say: "This is the most supportive learning atmosphere I've ever experienced. I would recommend taking classes to anyone. It's never too late." Another had to do with a 92-year-old gentleman from Curry County who, 78 years after dropping out of high school, decided to get a high school diploma. In 1918, at the age of 14, Joe Smith dropped out of school to go to work. When a friend said: "Joe, my goodness but you're getting old" Joe responded: "No, I'm not. I've just lived a lot longer than a lot of people." [56] Bill Dillingham, the GED instructor, said that Joe was definitely the oldest student he had ever had in his class!

From 1967 through 2009, 6,872 adults took and passed the GED exam as administered by SWOCC. Data from the earlier years is lost to history, but over the past ten years, 90 percent of those who passed the GED test had enrolled at the College to prepare themselves to take the exam (see Appendix).

As a direct result of the recession, President Ronald Reagan created several government sponsored programs to help retrain workers who had lost their jobs.

This in turn upped the number of students on campus, but also increased the average age of the student body on campus – not just at SWOCC, but nationwide.

In response, the College administration took aggressive action by putting more resources into the Developmental Education Program. They created more classes in basic writing, reading, study and math skills for these new students in order to help them reach college level coursework. In the beginning, enrolling in these remedial classes carried a pretty heavy stigma, so it took time for the program to get accepted. According to one faculty member, another benefit of the Developmental Ed Program was that it allowed the faculty members to raise the bar of their teaching in the traditional freshman and sophomore classes to a

The long registration line at SWOCC – 1980.

higher level. As such, the completion of an Associate of Arts degree was taking students three years to complete, not because the finish line was changed, but because the students weren't ready when they started. Registration now took longer as tests were administered to determine how best to assist the new students to become successful at college.

While it took more time for many of the students to "come up to speed" for college level work, the good news was that the Developmental Ed Program was providing high school level skills to its students. The programs also helped negotiations with the four-year colleges' Articulation Agreements (Coordination Agreements) by demonstrating that SWOCC's degree graduates were indeed prepared to enter a university as a junior. In 1987, the Oregon Legislature stepped forward and passed HB 2913 in an effort to eliminate - or at least ease - the politics in transferring course credits between the community colleges and the seven universities within the State. The new law directed "cooperation between the university system and community colleges on issues affecting student transfers – either to the university or from the university back to the community colleges." As such, a student with an Associate of Arts/Oregon Transfer degree (AAOT) from SWOCC had a guarantee that he or she would be admitted as a full-fledged junior at any of the seven universities within the State.[85] Similar articulation agreements, while not required by law, were made with local high schools where qualified seniors could take college level courses for credit.

The College tried to build a stronger link to the local high schools in an effort to get them to set higher standards for graduation and discipline. Still, the high school graduates that enrolled at the College were woefully ill-prepared for the rigors of college life. To that issue Professor Bower responded:

> *"We were good, maybe terrific, at taking ill-prepared students and bringing them up to college standards. The four-year schools did not do this as they had much higher entrance requirements on the S.A.T. exam and we filled the vacuum admirably!"*

In 1986, for instance, Powers High School joined forces with the College to provide distance learning classes in electronics and secretarial procedures via telecommunication. It was one of the first schools in the State to try a telecommunications project with a community college. While rudimentary by today's standards of e-learning, this was one of the first steps in providing video outreach teaching connections between the College and outlying towns within the district. As reported in the Myrtle Point Herald: [67]

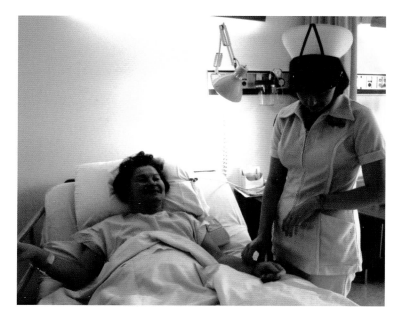

> *"Like a scene out of a futuristic movie, a small group of students watch an invisible hand draw the next lesson on a glass screen while a distant voice issues verbal directions and questions. Finally one of the students speaks into a small box and seconds later the voice congratulates the group on the correct answer. In this small corner of the Powers High School, the blackboard is replaced by a large television screen and the teacher is a small white box where two-way communication between the SWOCC electronics instructor and the students happen."*

While the demand for forest technicians and electricians was declining, other technical programs were on the rise. For instance, early in the decade, Bay Area Hospital requested that SWOCC expand the nursing program on campus. The College Board of Education agreed and expanded the incoming class by twelve students. At that time, students in the program had three levels of achievement options: (1) with three months of training, the student could qualify to work as a nurse's aide; (2) completion of four terms of study qualified a graduate for a Practical Nursing Certificate; and (3) completing the entire two-year program made the graduate eligible to take an examination to become a registered nurse. The request from the Hospital stated that without increasing the size of the nursing program at the College, they would have difficulty staffing the

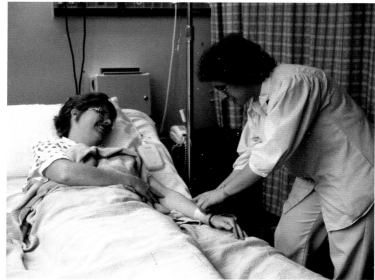

Student nurses getting advanced training with real patients at Bay Area Hospital in Coos Bay.

hospital's new patient wing. The relationship between the College's nursing program and the Hospital remains very strong today.

One of the goals of President Barber was to give SWOCC a bigger presence in the Coos Bay downtown area. President Barber is best remembered as a "system's manager." While Brookins focused on building the campus, Barber focused on organization and delivery of effective education. Barber was also very focused on using the College's resources to assist small businesses in the area. In October 1990, the College leased a part of the Hall Building and established the "Downtown Center" where Adult Basic Education and adult workforce re-entry assistance programs were taught under the auspices of Workforce 2000. In addition, the Business Development Center (BDC) was moved from the fifth floor of Tioga Hall to the Hall Building in order to make it more available to the business community to assist employers and employees with training programs. Both programs created additional FTE credit for the College in its continued quest for State funds.

Fitting this many projectors in your living room could be tricky, especially since it requires a 30 foot wide screen. Obviously, technology has come a long way since this "high tech" synchronized projection system was first introduced at SWOCC.

One of the most successful courses at the BDC was the Business Management Program; over the period from 1992-2008, well over 200 area businesses received intensive management and business development assistance. Shortly after Dr. Steve Kridelbaugh became president of the College, he closed the Downtown Center and built the Newmark Center where similar programs were provided.

The administration continually sought ways to draw the community into the campus. One of the ways to accomplish this was to provide things that were unique to the local citizens and something they might not experience otherwise. The multi-media film festival was one of those special events. It was started by Shirley Bridgham in 1982. Essentially it was a multi-projection slide presentation utilizing a synchronized projector/sound system that merged art, photography, music and electronics. It was high tech at the time and certainly was not simply a slide show. It required a screen 30 feet wide to handle the multiple projections and a synchronizer to coordinate the many projectors.

Another factor altering the social fabric of southern Oregon during the 1980s was the immigration of young retirees from California. Single family home prices in southern California shot through the roof during the prior decade, allowing homeowners to cash in on their equity, pay off any outstanding debts and head north for greener pastures. Once arriving in Oregon, they found bigger homes of higher quality at half the price as those left back in California. The demand was outstripping the supply and buyers even offered more than the seller's asking price in order to insure they got the home of their choice. This in turn priced many of the younger local buyers out of the market and drove the cost of an average home beyond the reach of many local people.

Why was this an issue for SWOCC? It was an issue for two reasons. First, many of the newcomers were retired, had already raised their children and were - as they say - "empty nesters." The reader should recall that during the 1980s the majority of school funding came directly from property tax assessments within the district. Since the assessed values were being driven upward by aggressive home pricing, the property taxes grew proportionally – often a bit of a shock to the Californians! This might suggest a larger amount of revenue available to school districts, including SWOCC. However, a reverse reaction occurred. While taxes were rising, local property owners, frustrated by the level of their property taxes, were voting down school levies that were above the annual increase of 6% as set by Oregon's Constitution. One might say that the new home buyers had not studied the Oregon property tax rules very carefully!

The other result of the immigration of retirees moving into the College district and the migration of family wage earners out of the district was the loss of income tax at the State level. Why? Because the family wage job was generally connected to some type of manufacturing operation that had closed or was "downsizing." The State, therefore, had received income taxes from both the employee as well as from the employer. The retirees, on the other hand, may have had a net worth exceeding the union worker at the mill, but much of their income producing assets were left back in California invested in stocks, bonds and CDs. These would be taxed in Oregon at a much reduced rate. The combination of these factors left the State coffers a bit short of revenue to distribute. Even though the State's proportion of the College's funding was less than 50% of its operations during the '80s, it was still very significant.

A happy mom holding her son and degree from SWOCC!

A third problem often overlooked in school funding was the amount of local property taxes paid by the large corporations that had giant milling operations within the district. Many of these operations also had a massive amount of timberland supporting the mill that was also taxed. These were all part of the property tax equation impacting SWOCC.

Since both local property tax receipts and income taxes collected by the State go to fund the College, SWOCC soon found itself in a financial bind. Obviously with the family wage earners losing their jobs and moving out of the area, the revenue sent to SWOCC from Salem began to drop. In addition to the FTE funding distributed to the College for operational costs, the majority of money that supported new building construction on the campus came via the State coffers, so there was precious little construction going on at SWOCC between 1983 and 1990. In fact, the new buildings on campus constructed during the decade were the result of a bond issue passed by the voters in 1979. President Brookins was only two years away from retirement and essentially completed his "mark" on the campus, and President Barber took over while the recession was in full swing.

Budgets during the 1980s were always an issue and tensions would rise between the Board of Education, the administration and the faculty/classified unions. One example, however, points out that even under difficult circumstances, levity can play a role. Bill Lemoine, professor of forestry, explained:

"We were surveying on campus and the forestry students were hacking out a clear line of sight with machetes for the compass man. Word was circulating about repairing and restricting the use of the school van used by the forestry club due to budget issues. The students got all upset and said to me 'you go and talk to the president (Jack Brookins) and get the decision reversed.' So off I went late in the afternoon straight from the field. I went up to the president's office, marched in and began talking to him about the issue. Unbeknownst to me, 12 of my surveying students had followed me up to the 5th floor of Tioga Hall – all carrying machetes and stood right behind me in Jack's office as I asked for a different decision. Jack said he would take it under consideration. He called me the next day and said he would reverse the decision, but said, 'Bill, you don't have to use that much pressure on me on future budget issues.'"

Moms registering for college.

Asked to comment on the culture of the campus during the 1980s, Professor Bob Bower said:

"The 1980s saw an increase in women on campus who were also supporting families. These women – often single mothers that were in their late '20s or early '30s - were amazing students and they had a profound effect on the classroom and the campus. The College, in conjunction with Head Start, provided day-care facilities on campus so they could attend classes during the day. They were much better at playing the role of a student. They weren't as distracted by athletics as men and usually the women did what they were asked to do. If you check the record of student awards, you will see that in the '80s the recipients were dominated by women, who were working, raising a family and going to school. They set a new standard!"

Professor Barbara Dodrill confirmed the notion that there was an increase in the number of women on campus during the 1980s. She spoke with pride when she talked about how she could see the impact of campus life on building the confidence of these young mothers. Ms. Dodrill remarked that she and Professor Helen Ferguson talked about this one day:

"It was such a joy to see these women come in to class on the first day all hunched over with not a shred of confidence and by the end of the year, they had their heads high and obviously feeling good about themselves."

The recession of the 1980s caused a lot of social unrest across the nation as family dynamics often turned ugly. Employment in Coos County was dropping quickly and families were searching for ways to make ends meet. Divorce was on the rise and mothers often found themselves without financial support in the home. It was not uncommon for the women of the 1960s and '70s to be homemakers and never really venture outside the home for employment. Veneita Stender recalled several instances where it was obvious that some of her older home economics students were coming from battered homes and something needed to be done.

Due to the efforts of Professor Stender, in 1985 the College was awarded a $250,000 grant through the Carl Perkins Vocational Education program specifically designed to help single-parent homemakers prepare themselves for employment or enter into college classes. The program was called the Single Parent-Displaced Homemaker course that later integrated into the Workforce Skills Center, then along with the JOBS Program integrated with Adult Basic Education into the Adult Learning Skills Program. Today, this area is known as the Transitional Education area.

According to Stender, the program also helped those less fortunate learn to budget and make their own clothes. Some of the students did not have much in the way of a home life to practice the cooking and home economic skills Stender was teaching. This was yet another example of how the College reached out into the community, assessed a need and rose to meet the challenge.

A report contained in the 30th anniversary campus newspaper tells yet another story as to why SWOCC is so special:

> *"One of the most telling moments of the decade (1980s), came at a graduation ceremony. A SWOCC student who had completed her program was called up the stage to receive her diploma; she was blind. Climbing the stairs she was accompanied by the guide dog that had been by her side through every step of her college years. The dog, too, was given a special diploma along with a particularly delicious dog biscuit. At this point, the ceremony stopped; 1,500 people in the audience looked on with moist eyes as the dog slowly crunched on his reward before escorting the new graduate off the stage. They had witnessed a heart-warming demonstration of the campus culture."*

Ms. Janet Cotner, a transfer student from Coquille, had her thoughts about SWOCC printed on the cover of the summer term class schedule of 1989:

> *"When I decided on a career, I jumped into school wholeheartedly with my goal firmly in mind. I didn't want to waste any time, so I made sure all the classes I'm taking are transferable. I'll be able to enter Brigham Young University next year as a junior. The school and people (at SWOCC) have made the transition from high school to college easier for me – giving me time to mature and to ease into the responsibilities of an independent college student."*

Or as Scott Lenhart, "a voc-ed" student from Coos Bay, put it:

> "At SWOCC I've been able to benefit from more experienced fellow students. After I get my two-year degree in automotive technology, I would like to work for one of the major automotive manufacturers. SWOCC is a great opportunity for me to get a quality education from instructors who are using the latest technology."

A bit earlier in the decade, *The World* newspaper asked four students what they would like to say about SWOCC:

> *Marcia Wood, a widowed mom from Arago:* "My kids are real proud of what I'm doing and what I've accomplished over there (SWOCC). I don't know what I'd done if the College hadn't been there. It was a real life-saver for me."

> *Sean Maidian:* "It's very personal there (SWOCC), and there is a lot of one-on-one relationships between the student and the teacher. The expense of the community college has also appealed to me. I work on weekends and live at home so I can afford to go to college. If there was no SWOCC, I would probably not be in college."

> *Jeff Town, Reedsport:* "In my first year, I enrolled in the automotive program, but then changed my mind and decided to focus my attention on a degree in engineering. That's the one thing about SWOCC, if you decide like I did to switch majors it's not as expensive as those four-year schools and you haven't lost a lot of money."

> *Diana Larsen:* "I know I had to have a degree to be employable. I'll get that degree next year at SWOCC just minutes from my home where I've still got three children to take care of."

In 1980, the enrollment at SWOCC was 5,417 students - 29% were from the age group 20-29 years old, followed by 23% aged 30-39 years old; close behind them was the over 50 crowd at 19%. Several state and federal programs were initiated to help "retrain" the out of work woods workers, and the College saw a dramatic rise in older students during the decade. Again, the College faced many new challenges during the decade. At the end of the decade the federal minimum wage was $3.35 per hour.

THE BUILDING YEARS - II

In the fall of 1990, Dr. Steve Kridelbaugh took over the reins of the College as its fourth president. Dr. Kridelbaugh was the top pick out of some 90 applicants to replace Dr. Bob Barber who left to become president of Central Oregon Community College in Bend, Oregon. According to Kridelbaugh, to be the president of a college like SWOCC was considered a real "plum" in the administrative world of academia. Prior to coming to SWOCC, he was the president of a small community college in Illinois, but he wanted to get back to the Pacific Northwest. The fit with SWOCC was a good one; but unbeknownst to him was the fact that a taxpayer revolt was about to storm across Oregon that would change the economics of running the campus forever – surprise!

When Dr. Kridelbaugh first visited the SWOCC campus earlier that spring, he said his first impression was "beautiful." The buildings were architecturally pleasing, the landscape was well done, and there was even a lake or two on campus. Furthermore, the College was just about to celebrate its 30th anniversary and he could participate almost immediately in the celebration, acknowledging the fact that 128,971 students had enrolled at the College over the past three decades – none of which he could take credit for!

Why, the interviewer asked, was the presidency of SWOCC such a real "plum"? "Well," as Kridelbaugh put it so succinctly, "look at the math." The Oregon Legislature had provided that the budget at a college could go up 6% per year without taxpayer approval. For argument sake, let's say that the State and federal governments kicked in 30% of the operating costs of running the College, the local property taxes contributed 50% and tuition and fees accounted for the rest. This meant there was a guaranteed 6% increase in 50% of the College's budget paid by the local property tax portion without any further action on the part of the College administration or the taxpayer. "That was really something," stated Kridelbaugh. So in his mind, this was a terrific opportunity to lead a college without a lot of administrative headaches surrounding funding. Of course that was all before Ballot Measure 5 kicked in. We'll get to that story in just a moment, but first let's pause to enjoy the first 30-year celebration of SWOCC.

On the national front, the decade of the 1990s again saw the American military in action – the first Gulf War, Somalia, Haiti, Bosnia, and Yugoslavia – as the United States played arbitrator, enforcer, and peacekeeper throughout the world.

The draft had been eliminated (but draft registration was still required), so the military was all voluntary and not a hot topic on campus. The decade might also be characterized by the collapse of the Soviet Union and the end of the Cold War. The dot-com bubble, cell phones, the World Wide Web (www), the introduction and proliferation of e-mail, e-commerce and caller I.D. all joined together to ramp up American technology. South Africa and Nelson Mandela, Princess Di, the Chicago Bulls and Michael Jordan, Au Pair, Dolly the cloned sheep, the Hubble telescope with its images from Mars and Saturn, Tiger Woods, Y2K and Viagra all became household words.

It was appropriate that SWOCC held the celebration of its 30th birthday in the International Woodworkers of America (IWA) Union hall in North Bend, Oregon because they, along with the International Longshore and Warehouse Union, were the backbone of getting the College started.

Fashions were a dichotomy as young people continued their quest for individuality. It could even be said the decade was one of "anti-fashion" as a backlash to the opulence of the 1980s. On one hand, some young men wore what might be called the "preppie" look while others wore larger and larger jeans that hung on their hips lower and lower – baggie might be the operative word and the droopier the better. Chains and black leather with colored hair characterized the "Nu-Metal" genre. Tattoos and body piercing were in vogue. Music on campus was a split between Hip Hop and Rap or Country and Western with the likes of Garth Brooks. Oddly, the younger teens of this decade often preferred to listen to the music of their parents – a new fad, or was it a revival of an old fad?

Some of the language of the 1990s: [34]

Bama –	a redneck or ultra conservative
Beans –	money
Bones –	money
Chick-flick –	a movie girls would like
Going postal –	going crazy
I'm gone –	good bye
To jack –	to steal something
Not! –	a function word at the end of the sentence reversing the meaning
Po Po –	police
So! –	an intensifying adverb usually at the beginning of a statement
Sweet –	really nice or cool
Wacked –	crazy
Whatever –	clueless

Political gossip again raged at the highest level of the U.S. government as President Bill Clinton was accused by several women of sexual misconduct. He narrowly survived an impeachment trial to remove him from office for perjury and obstruction of justice. O.J. Simpson, once the hero of the gridiron, was placed on trial after being accused of killing his wife and her friend. And the ill-fitting black glove convinced the jury of his innocence as news pundits offered their own spectrum of truths.

Race riots would continue and international terrorism would rear its ugly head with the bombing of the Federal building in Oklahoma City by a citizen of our own country – Timothy McVey. Terror would also strike the nation's schools, the worst of which was the shootings at Columbine High School in Littleton, Colorado. The "welfare to work" programs were initiated in an attempt to break the addiction to government programs that discouraged people from finding a job. It didn't work, but it was a valiant try. The economy was in high gear during the '90s with unemployment averaging 5.75%.

Such was not the case in southwestern Oregon as the final blow to the forest products dominated economy was delivered by two small innocent birds – the Northern Spotted Owl and the Marbled Murrelet. The 1990s was a sobering decade for dozens of small towns and for the thousands involved in logging and lumbering throughout the northwest. The door was finally closed on the boom time for the forest products industry. Shrill voices decried the Endangered Species Act of 1973 and charged that spotted owls and marbled murrelets were not worth the loss of jobs and payrolls.

For reference purposes, Coos, Curry and Douglas Counties have more federal and state-owned forest land within their boundaries than any other region of the nation. As such, the national forest policies made in Washington, D.C. concerning these lands have the greatest employment impact on these three counties than anywhere else in the country. Hence the direct impact on SWOCC.

As a direct result of these policies, on August 29, 1990, management at the Georgia Pacific (G.P.) plywood plant in Coquille announced the permanent closure of the 54-year old mill, effective the day after Labor Day. This action put 340 workers "on the street" almost overnight. It was reported that this was the largest single mill closure in Oregon. Joe Muenzer, a 59-year-old man who had worked at the mill for 25 years, was dismayed, discouraged and numb: "I can hardly retire; I've got a wife and house payments. I'll have to do something."

SWOCC immediately entered the fray to offer its resources. College employees Brenda Brecke, director of the Workforce 2000 program at the Skills Center in downtown Coos Bay, and Ann Fauss, counselor, stepped in to provide guidance in directing the dislocated workers toward new career counseling and courses on the campus. Computers and programs were set up in the Union Hall in Coquille to assist with the counseling. As a direct result of their personal involvement, 118 of the dislocated G.P. workers came to college seeking a new direction for their lives. It must have been emotionally draining for the SWOCC counselors to listen to the heart-wrenching stories of the dislocated workers. Dr. Kridelbaugh also told the unemployed workers from the Mill that the first 100 of them that enrolled in a class at the College would have their tuition waived; 90 of them enrolled – yet another example of the compassion the College has shown the community. [80] The Workforce 2000 group continued to work to assist employees impacted by mill closures from Reedsport to Brookings.

In an explanation of the economic conditions that began a decade earlier, the Oregon Employment Department explained what was meant by structural unemployment, one of the major issues facing Coos, Curry and Douglas residents:

> *"Structural unemployment is caused by a mismatch between the types of jobs available and the skills of workers and may be the most serious type of unemployment. Barriers to matching jobs to workers may come from such sources as the modification in the area's economic base (e.g., a change from wood products to service industries) or through technological change. Structural unemployment is a problem that does not go away after a recession ends as might be the case with cyclical unemployment. Basically, people affected by structural unemployment are not just out of jobs, they are out of careers."*

The impact of these mill closures throughout the College district was significant. As mentioned, when the major mills dismantled their operations, the property taxes associated with these facilities went from considerable to essentially zero. And the out-migration of family wage jobs caused the real estate property values to plummet severely, reducing the assessed value and consequent drop in property tax revenue for the College.

For comparative purposes and to illustrate the difficulty faced in funding the operating costs at the College, the average per capita income in Coos County in the early '90s was around $12,000 per year, $2,000 lower than the State average of $14,000 and nearly $4,000 lower than the national average. About 18% of the district population had incomes below the federal poverty level; over 37% of the female head of household families were living below the poverty level, nearly double the percentage of total families living below the poverty level.

At one point during the decade, Coos County had the highest unemployment rate and was the most depressed county in the entire nation; not a trophy one wants to have! On the flip side, the demand for social services and for training at the College increased as the displaced workers sought retraining. It was about this time that the current president, Dr. Patty Scott, was hired as the director of Student Support Services to create programs that focused on the needs of first generation – low income students, particularly with the goal of retaining those students enrolled on campus. The first class offered was on how to be a college student. As the '90s unfolded, the recession of the 1980s continued to deepen in Coos, Curry and Douglas Counties and yet the demand for basic student programs increased on campus. Statistics at the time continued to demonstrate that 50% of college level freshmen could not do college level English/writing and 80% could not do college level math – both the adults seeking retraining and the new 18-year old high school graduates. Coincidentally, the focus on keeping students enrolled at the College also helped with the FTE calculation.

In 1989, Salem responded to the impending problem when the Economic Development Department issued "Oregon Shines" as its strategic plan. The plan committed "Oregon to provide the best educated and trained workforce in the United States by the year 2000 and a workforce competitive with any other country in the world by 2010." Did we make it? Probably not, but the Legislature responded that same year to the Department by passing the Workforce 2000 Act. The community skills centers were first funded under this Act and SWOCC was one of four colleges selected for executing this plan. The College would take on the challenge of bringing the workforce forward to meet the goal of Oregon Shines.

At the national level, the 24-hour sports channels made their way into the American living rooms, and more people than ever before watched their favorite players apply their special talents. Michael Jordan would dominate the decade in basketball and Cal Ripkin would play out his magnificently long career on the diamond. The San Francisco 49ers would continue their dynasty as one of the best teams in football, finally giving way to Brett Favre and the Green Bay Packers.

On the education front, Congress passed the Elementary and Secondary Education Act (No Child Left Behind) that provided assistance to disadvantaged students with limited proficiency in English as well as improving the instruction in areas such as math, science and reading. Advanced college courses could be taken "online" and - for better or worse - distance learning became commonplace. By decade's end, 83% of the population in America had completed high school vs. just 41% back in the1960s. Undoubtedly, distance learning and online classes delivered by community colleges across the nation have helped these statistics.

The student profile during the fall term of 1990-91 gives some indication of the composition of the students that enrolled at SWOCC. The mix of students on campus had done a complete 180 degree change from the student body profile of 30 years earlier:

Total Students Served	4,646	
In-District Students Enrolled	3,753	(81%)
Male	1,912	(41%)
Female	2,734	(59%)
Traditional Students (18-21 years old)	636	(14%)
Median Age of Students	37	
Full-Time Students (12+ credits)	625	(13%)
Part-Time Students	4,021	(87%)

While one might argue that the 1990s decade was not the low point in the economy of Coos, Douglas and Curry Counties when compared to the deep national recession of the upcoming decade, the 1990s were a very difficult time for SWOCC. The community enrollment in the vocational programs on campus was greatly diminished as the demand for electronic technicians, electricians, forestry technicians and the like were a casualty of the shattered local economy. Most of the local mills were closed and shuttered and in some cases the property use had completely changed. The community continued to drift with no real leadership or vision.

Let's return for the moment to the funding issues for the College. In the late 1980s a groundswell of tax revolt was beginning to take shape across Oregon; it had been simmering for years and it finally exploded in 1990. A new law was passed on November 6, 1990 by the voters of Oregon. It would determine the way public schools, including community colleges, would be funded in Oregon. It was called Ballot Measure 5 and it modified Article 11 Section 11 of the Oregon Constitution. Under this amendment, local property taxes dedicated to school funding were capped at $15 per $1,000 of market value assessment in the beginning and, after a five-year phase-in, was lowered to a maximum $5 per thousand of assessed value.

The main argument supporting the passage of Measure 5 lay in the fact that school districts with higher valued property under the previous system could fund local schools at a higher rate than more economically depressed areas. To offset this reduction in local funding, the major responsibility for school funding was transferred from local property taxes to the State's general fund in order to equalize revenue among school districts. A formula was devised that distributed funds to schools based upon the number of Full-Time Equivalent students (FTE). As the economy of Oregon has contracted, Measure 5 has been blamed for the funding ills of every school district throughout the State.

The tax revolt did not end with Measure 5. In November 1996 Measure 47 was passed that restricted the way local property assessments could be increased. It fixed the assessed value of private property at the lesser of 1994-95 or 1995-96 values, and those values could be increased by no more than 3% per year by the local county assessor. Measure 47 also put in place a very difficult hurdle for the State to overcome in order to change the way property taxes were modified. It was called the double majority rule for other than general elections and required a turnout of more than 50% of the registered voters in a district – an almost impossible level to achieve. Measure 5 changed the structure of school funding, Measure 47 limited the growth of local property taxes and how they might be modified. Measure 47 impacted all taxing budgets in the State from cities, counties, fire districts, school districts and other special districts. No one was exempt. But that is not the end of the story.

A year later, sufficient signatures were collected by petition to place yet another property tax limitation ballot before the voters. It was known as Measure 50 and under this law, each school district - including community colleges - was assigned a permanent, fixed property tax base for school operations that could not be increased by the local governing boards. The old 6% annual increase in school budgets in Oregon was "out the window" as were the old local "override tax levies." Measure 50 corrected some of the technical issues inherent in Measure 47, but maintained the 3% limitation on property value assessment growth. As it turned out, this was hardly enough to keep up with inflation. When coupled with the migration of family wage jobs out of the State and the constitutional requirement that the Governor balance the Oregon budget each year, education was in for some tough sledding. [42]

Why is this discussion important to this book on the 50th anniversary celebration of SWOCC? The impact of these three Measures and the reshaping of the State's economy limited the way educators in Oregon could meet their funding needs and directly impact their programs. In summary, it shifted the emphasis on how the College funding would operate in the future. Shortfalls in funding would cause significant problems for college presidents who were responsible for balancing the College budgets. In summary:

1. Property taxes that once were the major financial support for the College campus were now reduced to about 25% of the cost of operations;

2. The general fund at the State level became the major source of funding for the College and would ebb and flow with the overall economy of the State, regardless of what might be happening in the College's own district;

3. The number of family wage earners within the district had been dramatically reduced because of the recession that has lasted for the past 30 years;

4. The percentage of "traditional students" that were ready for college level work was slipping as the funding for local K-12 dropped;

5. There was a marked increase in older people within the district, not simply due to the normal aging of the residents, but the immigration into the district of retired people moving from California;

6. The number of part-time students seeking retraining in order to find a different type of employment had increased, requiring the same level of administrative support without the corresponding local employment of the graduate; and

7. Tuition increases at SWOCC were impacting those who were living day to day from unemployment insurance payments or other government sponsored programs and simply could not afford to pay the higher costs of going to college.

All of these were important to the overall financial health of the College and indirectly to the quality of education made available to all school districts including K-12 and universities. Funding education and how to get it became "front and center" for all educators across the State. It exacerbated the problem of high school graduates being ill prepared for college level work.

As Dr. Steve Kridelbaugh explained in his interview for this book, a drive for funding became practically the sole focus of administrators of public educational institutions, not just SWOCC. Fiscal reductions in State support for higher education prompted Oregon's universities to raise admission standards and increase tuition, thus closing the doors to many promising but underprepared students. Stopping their pursuit of education was one option, but many turned to the community colleges for help. Kridelbaugh was determined to accommodate those students, but any new program introduced at SWOCC would have to "pay for itself," as there was no cushion left in the coffers. The job of the college president shifted from managing education to funding it. Further complicating the funding issue facing the College's future was the bleak outlook concerning the number of K-12 students within the SWOCC district. From 1990 to 2009, the ten school districts within the College district saw their enrollment drop from 15,102 students to 11,008 – a drop of 27% in 20 years. The change in the employment picture within southwestern Oregon was going to have a dramatic impact on the College. This certainly did not bode well for the future funding of the College and forced Dr. Kridelbaugh to look beyond the district boundaries for new FTE.

Kridelbaugh turned to John Speasl, the athletic director at the College, for help in recruiting more out-of-district student-athletes to SWOCC. Speasl "signed on" and began an aggressive recruiting campaign. Toward the end of the decade, the College built one of the best training rooms in Prosper Hall of any community college in the country and started an "athletic trainer program" on campus that consistently has 30 students enrolled. Out of the average population of student-athletes during the decade of around 200 per year, 70% came from outside the State. It seemed that having excellent sports programs added considerably to the College's ability to build FTE.

An odd, yet creative scenario happened as community colleges sought ways to offset the loss in local revenues and further tap into the State's reimbursement for FTE. It all started with Treasure Valley Community College in Ontario, Oregon. Their college district touched the Idaho state boundary and through a quirk in the Oregon statutes, Treasure Valley Community College was able to bring students, who were residents of Idaho, to their campus at in-district tuition rates and have them count as Full-Time Equivalent students for Oregon FTE reimbursement purposes. Other community colleges along the Columbia River quickly followed suit by lobbying the Legislature to allow them the same privilege.

In essence, Oregon taxpayers were footing much of the bill to provide two years of college education for non-residents of Oregon. In some cases, even tuition fees were waived. Obviously, this was patently unfair to those community colleges whose districts lay entirely within the center of Oregon!

In response, SWOCC, along with other community colleges whose district borders did not touch a neighboring state, lobbied the Legislature about the unfairness of this proposition. They won their argument and all community colleges within Oregon could now bring in students from Washington, Idaho, California and Nevada for in-district tuition rates and have them count as FTE for State funding. Dr. Kridelbaugh commented:

> *"About 85% of my time during my 15-year tenure as president of SWOCC was spent trying to protect the funding base of the College in order to keep it financially viable."*

That was true for all colleges within the State – community colleges and universities alike.

With the passage of the property tax limitations, marketing to recruit students became a major effort of each community college in Oregon. Alaska became a productive recruiting ground for SWOCC. Concurrently, the College had created several new sports programs specifically designed to increase enrollment and boost FTE. There was another interesting factor that played into this strategy; a student from Alaska who lived in Oregon for three months could be considered a resident of Oregon and therefore qualify for in-district tuition rates, often in their first quarter of study. Since there were no community colleges per se in Alaska, SWOCC became a home for many of their high school graduates – particularly their athletes. As a direct result of Dr. Kridelbaugh's vision and entrepreneurial approach to funding the growth of the College, the number of athletic teams on campus almost tripled overnight. And it also placed heavier class loads on the traditional academic courses, which became a subject of contention between the administration and the faculty.

In addition to recruiting students from the states bordering Oregon (plus Alaska), an effort was launched by the College to bring international students to SWOCC. While State funding was unavailable for these students, the fees amounted to more than $5,000 per student per year, well in excess of the marginal costs of providing these services. This helped offset some of the general operating costs for the in-district residents. Students from various countries, including

Japan, Korea, China and South Vietnam, began coming to SWOCC. When student housing first became available, the goal was to get 50 international students onto the campus by providing "dorm" space and a meal plan for them. The foreign students seemed to fit in fairly well and were mixed in with the local students. Most of them stayed on campus for the full two years primarily to increase their English language skills before going on to a four-year university. After September 11, 2001, the population of international students on campus declined for the balance of the decade as it became much more difficult to get student visas.

It is probably time to divert attention away from the political environment of running SWOCC and shift attention to what was happening to the building footprint on campus. Suffice to say that in the tradition of President Jack Brookins, Dr. Kridelbaugh was not going to let the sluggish local economy, the tax revolt or the problems in Salem interrupt the vision to expand the campus – both in size and in quality. The first building added to the campus in the '90s was Stensland Hall; it would house the bookstore, counseling center and classrooms. The building was

Construction begins on Stensland Hall – under the watchful eye of Henry Hansen – December 1994.

Stensland Hall was the first building on campus named for an individual (Don Stensland, retired geology professor) and not one of the defunct post offices within the College district.

Stensland Hall completed.

The initial clearing of the baseball diamond – June 1996.

Sand and drainage rock were hauled in to make the diamond usable – October 1996.

SWOCC baseball diamond nearing completion – April 1997.

funded out of College reserves, the sale of a building the College owned in downtown Empire, plus a $315,000 loan that was paid back from profits from the bookstore.

Just after the completion of Stensland Hall, the College undertook a project to build a full-sized baseball field just north of the fire training tower. The College's contribution of $100,000 for the project along with donations by the National Guard and local citizens resulted in a first-class hardball diamond.

The success of recruiting students from outside the College district meant the students needed someplace to live. Funded and supported by the College Foundation, Dr. Kridelbaugh's staff conducted a study of all the community colleges throughout the nation that had student housing – there were about 160 in total. From the 110 surveys that were returned, it became obvious to Dr. Kridelbaugh that each president of a community college that had student housing raved about the absolute necessity for providing student housing on campus and, in most cases, indicated they were moneymakers.

In early 1996, after evaluating this information, the College contracted with Heery International (a respected construction management firm) to develop a scope of work and design criteria for a student housing complex on campus. Three directors from the College Board of Education were assigned to the Finance Committee to review and recommend financing options for the project. In September of that year, the Board convened a special meeting to review the recommendations and the proposals submitted by three architectural firms.

The team of Daniel Park and Associates (architect) with Adroit Construction (contractor) were selected and the Board authorized them to proceed with Phase One of the Student Housing project for a total cost not to exceed $3.6 million (including construction, landscaping, and furnishings). The College borrowed the money and simultaneously contributed $500,000 to a Student Housing Sinking Fund in the Insurance Reserve to cover any initial cost overruns. Nine new buildings were built under

Phase One. They all opened for fall term 1997 with full occupancy. There were 31 four-person apartments and two additional apartments for the Resident Assistants for a total capacity of 125 students.

The interior of each apartment was quite nice. Each apartment was about 1,200 square feet and had four-single occupancy bedrooms with a common living room, dining room and kitchen. Each building was named after Oregon lighthouses (as well as the historic depot that supplied U.S. lighthouses) – Lighthouse Depot, Tillamook Head, Umpqua River, Cape Meares, Cape Blanco, Cape Arago, Coquille River, Yaquina Head and Heceta Head. Credit goes to Barb Robson, an employee of the College at the time, for the suggestions on how best to name the buildings.

The student housing had to be carved out of the forest that surrounded the campus. Some members of the faculty saw the location of the student housing as a forest within which the student housing could be incorporated, while others were driven to get the maximum student housing capacity in place as soon as possible. This meant clearing the forest to make way for the units. The clearing of the land for Phase One started in 1996 and the first units were completed for the fall term of 1997.

With the demand for student housing increasing, in March 1998 the College Board of Education authorized two more student housing units to be constructed at a cost of around $840,000. The completion of Phase Two of the housing project added space for 40 more students and brought the total capacity of the student housing to 198 beds. [54]

A survey of the students living in these "dorms" indicated a desire to convert some of the Phase One units from single occupant bedrooms to double occupancy. The remodel was undertaken simultaneously with the Phase Two construction and converted 31 one-person rooms into 31 double occupancy units. These were designated as the "overflow" units. Phase Two units were named North Head and St. George Reef.

Student housing construction.

In the fall of 1999, as the third year of student housing on campus began, the demand for student quarters had risen to 250 paid applicants. The College utilized a nearby off-campus apartment complex to meet this new demand. In December 1999, the Board of Education approved Phase Three construction of four additional buildings with a capacity of 92 more beds, at a cost of $2 million. These units were named Warrior Rock, Willamette River, Point Adams and Desdemona Sands.

In the fall of 2004, the growth of the College dictated a fresh look at expanding the student housing program. Recruiting efforts were ongoing for both out-of-state students as well as bringing more international students onto the campus. The Oregon Coast Culinary Institute was also coming along and those students needed places to stay. A consultant was hired to evaluate the situation and their report to the Board indicated there was a need for increased bed capacity in the housing complex. In order to improve the density of beds per square foot, the consultant recommended three-story buildings be constructed vs. the older style two storied structures.

A detailed financial analysis was conducted and it was determined that Phase Four could create a positive cash flow and meet the necessary demand for housing with some extra capacity to address future growth. In 2004, the Board of Education approved bonding the College for an expenditure of $4.8 million to build four additional three-story units. They were named Trinidad Head, Battery Point, Gray's Harbor and Willapa Bay. This phase brought the total housing capacity to 396 residents (with room for an additional 31 students in the remodeled overflow doubles from Phase One). Some members of the community suggested Kridelbaugh was trying to move SWOCC from a two-year community college to a full-fledged four-year university. Most in the community could not see the importance of the student housing to the continued success of the College as chartered. Hindsight proved him right and the naysayers wrong!

The newer three-story student housing units on campus.

Parents of prospective students loved the idea of having their young student stay in a nice clean place with meal plans available and required. Once they saw the quality of the "dorms," the majority were sold on SWOCC. However, as the saying goes, "all that glitters is not gold." As the density of the students living in the units grew, there were some unexpected negative consequences associated with the housing program; specifically thefts, personal assaults and drug arrests increased on campus and posed new challenges for the College administration.

In an interview for this book, President Kridelbaugh summed up his thoughts about expanding the campus at Empire Lakes during his tenure:

> *"Put simply, by being fiscally conservative, by developing an entrepreneurial attitude and through private funding from the College's Foundation, buildings like the Hales Performing Arts Center got built. Some construction projects were funded by borrowing money to be amortized over time via the rental monies they produced – The Newmark and Family Center and student housing were classic examples."*

SWOCC became very creative in finding ways to increase the revenues flowing to the campus by thinking outside the proverbial box. In a letter to the community in 1999, President Kridelbaugh made the following observation: "If there is one word that could describe the changes at the College over the past five years, it would be growing." He was referring to the addition of Curry County to the College district on July 1, 1995, the building of Stensland Hall, the Newmark Center and Family Center, 11 student housing buildings, a baseball field, an athletic field house and soon to be constructed Performing Arts Center. From 1995 – 1999, 145,000 square feet of building space was added to the footprint of the campus at a capital cost of $15 million. In hindsight, that was a pretty impressive record and with the addition of Curry County, the SWOCC district covered 3,648 square miles stretching from Reedsport to the California state line.

As far as funding new operations or projects during the decade were concerned, Kridelbaugh was pretty blunt when he told the faculty and staff:

> *"If it wasn't at least cash neutral in the near term, it (any new program) was not going to get approved."*

Friction developed between the faculty and the administration over the perceived change in the focus of the College. On one hand, the academic faculty saw a huge effort put forth by the administration to create new athletic programs in order to attract more students from outside the district; consequently, more funding was required to accommodate the growing student body – more buildings were being built. In contrast, the increase in the number of students on campus meant heavier student loads in the traditional classes for the faculty without the requisite funding or salaries to make it all work. Class sizes increased while the support staff (classified) dropped. More responsibilities seemed to flow to the professional staff to teach more with less. As Professor Bower put it,

> *"It is difficult to put into words how the College changed. It seemed that education took a back seat to recruiting and the ubiquitous FTE."*

Had the College lost touch with the "community"? Yes and no. Originally, the College district taxpayers footed the majority of the cost of operating the campus programs and felt connected with the College. If they didn't like what was going on at SWOCC, their attitudes were simply expressed at the ballot box. After Measure 5 passed, and the new funding formula took hold, the relationship between the College and the community changed and not for the better. The

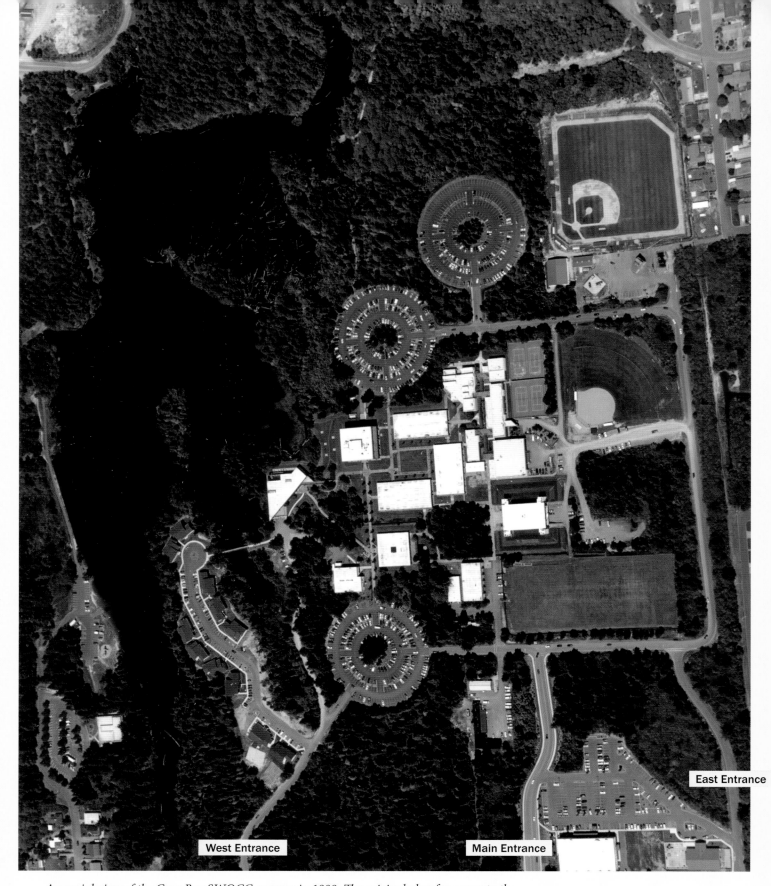

West Entrance **Main Entrance** **East Entrance**

An aerial view of the Coos Bay SWOCC campus in 1999. The original plan for access to the SWOCC campus called for an east and west entrance. In 1992, Wal-Mart began seeking permits for the construction of a shopping center on the south side of Newmark Avenue directly across from the College. Originally, there was a stoplight at the east entrance to the College, but that location was not conducive for traffic flow into Wal-Mart. The company requested that the Oregon Department of Transportation Highway Division place a traffic light at the main entrance to the Wal-Mart facility. Because the Highway Division would not approve locating a second traffic light on Newmark close to the existing traffic light located at the east entrance to the College campus, Wal-Mart, Inc., agreed to build a new college entrance. This became known as the main entrance to the campus.

administration, out of necessity, had to spend most of its time thinking of creative ways to boost the funding mechanisms to keep the College functioning and this meant thinking outside the College district boundaries to get more FTE enrolled. Competition for revenue to fund operations was the new currency of a college president.

One other factor that should be illuminated is the fact that the two major Oregon universities (U of O and OSU) started chasing their FTE by introducing a program called "Enrollment Enhancement." This program encouraged all students to spend their entire four years on the university campus in order to efficiently progress toward graduation, and creative incentives were added to make this strategy happen. One could easily conclude that this program was a ploy to move students away from the community college network directly to the university.

SWOCC responded by tailoring all of their college transfer classes and degree programs to match those of the universities; as mentioned earlier, this was called an "Articulation Agreement" and became part of the strategy to hold FTE on the SWOCC campus. These agreements essentially provided students with assurance that upon graduation from a community college where the course curriculum had been approved by a university, the student holding that degree could enter the university with full junior standing. SWOCC could then continue to market itself as a much cheaper way for a student to complete the first two years of college by living at home and paying in-district tuition rates.

Competition continued on another front between the University of Oregon and SWOCC for headcount. The University set up another program known as Correspondence Schools where seniors at a high school like Powers, for instance, could take a university level writing or math course in the evenings at the high school and get U of O college credit. The problem was that the Powers High teacher might not have the requisite college credentials to teach the college level class and/or might not follow the course outline verbatim. The University turned a blind eye to this minor requirement. Often the SWOCC professors were called upon to answer questions the instructor at the high school was ill prepared to handle; yet the U of O got the FTE head count credit! One begins to understand how funding mechanisms became the lead driver for school administrators and why student housing became an important strategy for SWOCC:

1. It provided affordable, accessible housing to students who attend SWOCC from outside of the College district;

2. It increased state-reimbursable FTE by attracting additional full-time students to the campus;

3. It improved the campus culture through greater participation in campus activities and programs resulting in greater retention of students;

4. It provided the opportunity to develop camps and conferences that utilize on-campus housing during the summer months;

5. It provided affordable, accessible housing to residents of the College district who live beyond reasonable commuting distance; and

6. It provided ready housing for employers who brought college interns to the community for summer employment.

On a lighter side, at the beginning of Dr. Kridelbaugh's tenure as president, he introduced a new program that would help insure future FTE growth at the College. In fact, each year of his tenure he would go to the local hospital to personally present a certificate to the first-born baby during Community College Month, in April. The certificate provided the child a tuition waiver for one year to attend SWOCC upon graduation from high school.

President Steve Kridelbaugh presents Ms. Katherine Marie Chambers with a certificate qualifying her for a one-year tuition waiver scholarship to Southwestern Oregon Community College as proud mother, Junia Chambers, looks on. Photo courtesy of The World newspaper.

Just as the need for the opportunity to gain access to a college education spurred Henry Hansen's drive to establish a community college on the South Coast, the increasing need for access to bachelor's and master's degrees spurred President Kridelbaugh to press for a "University Center" to serve the residents of the South Coast. The University Center was to serve as a bridge between the community college programs and the newly emerging outreach efforts of the State's universities. Its purpose was to connect place-bound residents of the South Coast region with the programs and services of the member institutions of the Oregon University System (OUS).

Meetings in the early- to mid-1990s between President Kridelbaugh and Oregon University System Chancellor Joe Cox explored the challenges faced by rural residents in completing a four-year degree and the potential for involving the community colleges which were dispersed around rural Oregon. At the same time, Central Oregon Community College President Bob Barber (former SWOCC president) began lobbying in earnest to bring a four year institution to Bend, Oregon. The two presidents attempted to gain the interest of the other community colleges in the concept to help gain the political backing of the Oregon University System and to persuade the Legislature to fund the centers.

The first "University Center" was formed at Central Oregon Community College in Bend in 1995. It took another three years and significant lobbying by President Kridelbaugh to persuade the Legislature to fund a second University Center at SWOCC, but eventually, in the summer of 1998, the Emergency Board approved funding the program at a cost of $200,000 annually, and the Southwestern Oregon University Center was sanctioned. At the time, Vice Chancellor Shirley Clark announced:

> *"We are very pleased to join with our partners at Southwestern in creating a new center whose mission will be expanding access to higher education services and outreach for residents of the region. Working together we expect*

to respond to market demands for a growing number of degree programs from OUS institutions that will be closely articulated with Southwestern's curriculum."

The College set aside office space on the third floor of Tioga Hall and a search went forth to find a program director. In January 1999, Dr. Andrew N. Duncan was appointed director. Vice Chancellor Clark went on to say:

"Southwestern is indeed fortunate to have someone with Andy's program and administrative experience and personal charm. His work as a superintendent of schools of the Gulf Islands School District in British Columbia and composed of numerous island schools, gives him unique insight into the issues to be faced in making access to higher education available to the widely dispersed population of the Oregon Coast."

By July 1999, the University Center was fully operational on campus with extensive networks established between several universities and the Center. The following academic year, 152 students on the South Coast took a total of 230 university courses for 38.83 FTE. As of July 2010, 48 different bachelor's, master's, and doctoral degree programs were available to students from the South Coast and two new degree programs were under development. The Center provided university course opportunities for 300-350 students and routinely graduated 20 – 50 students per year.

In 2000-2001, several new programs were introduced at the Center: an on-site teacher certification degree program operated by Eastern Oregon University; a Master of Business Administration (MBA) program by Portland State University; and one-time, grant funded Master of Science in Family Nurse Practitioner program from Oregon Health Sciences University (now Oregon Health & Science University).

In 2002, SWOCC allocated more space on the third floor of Tioga Hall to accommodate the growing teacher education program through Eastern Oregon University. The program was extremely popular and provided degrees in Elementary and Secondary Education, and today every elementary school from Florence to the California border boasts at least one graduate of the program. The continuing success of this initial licensure program led to the establishment of a master's degree and continuing licensure program offered by Southern Oregon University as a hybrid program with summer on-site courses in Coos Bay. This program traditionally enrolls 25 or more students in each of the summer classes.

Some of the programs, however, were a bit unusual – to say the least: the 2000 MBA program was an interesting one that consisted of videotaped lectures mailed weekly to the Center and supported by written assignments. Imagine, if you will, a group of students gathered together one long evening each week, lounging on the couches on the third floor of Tioga, eating pizza, drinking copious amounts of coffee and watching a week's worth of lectures on videotape until 1:00 in the morning!

In 2004, SWOCC came within a "hair's breadth" of losing the University Center as the State came face to face with the reality of a deepening economic recession. One of the casualties of the recession was the funding of university centers. President Kridelbaugh was faced with the daunting task of lobbying to get the Center funded. With assistance from influential community members, local politicians and prominent figures such as Senator Mark Hatfield, President Kridelbaugh worked with the Legislature and the State Board of Higher Education to reinstate the funding for the Center. The ultimate outcome was that the campus funding of the Center was restored, but the funding stream and the oversight of university centers was transferred to Eastern Oregon University. Even then, the funds were tight and budgets had to be reduced.

Notwithstanding the difficulties faced by the Center, it has continued to thrive and provide services to South Coast residents; between 2002 and 2010, 275 students graduated from SWOCC's University Center programs and the great majority – over 80% – have stayed on the South Coast.

Returning to the economic conditions within the College district for a moment, it is critically important to understand that the structured unemployment issues discussed earlier were not getting better. In fact, throughout the decade unemployment continued to worsen as more and more mills closed and many individuals slipped through the cracks. To help stem the tide, SWOCC made a large commitment by building the Newmark Center – a 35,000 square foot building that would house the One-Stop-Career-Center that was initially occupied in 1996.

In 1995, SWOCC formed a partnership with State agencies and non-profit organizations in the County to develop the Career and Opportunity One Stop program, and constructed a building on the south edge of the campus along Newmark Avenue to house the agencies. It became known as the Newmark Center. An additional building – the Family Center – was constructed next to the Newmark Center. The goal of the One Stop Center was to bring to one location those agencies that could help move individuals and families toward successful employment and self-sufficiency by providing integrated educational and support services under one roof. SWOCC's connection not only provided the facilities, but also ready access to instructors and classes. The Center serves dislocated workers, underemployed persons who want to train for a new career, displaced homemakers, and other adults who are prime candidates for continuing education.

Clearing the trees to make way for the Newmark Center – April 1995.

By November '95, the brush and trees had been removed and construction was about to begin.

The partners at the Newmark Center included:

Oregon Adult and Family Services; Southwestern Oregon Community Action; South Coast Business Employment; Oregon Employment Department; Retired and Senior Volunteer Program; Consumer Credit Counseling; Oregon Federal Credit Union; Bay Area Mediation Services; South Coast Head Start; Coos County Mental Health; Oregon Vocational Rehabilitation Division; Oregon Services to Children and Families; Oregon Commission for the Blind; Family Center for drop in child care; Green Thumb; North Bend Housing Authority; Personnel Solutions; Oregon Senior and Disabled Services and a variety of programs from the College.

The Newmark Center Mission Statement reads: "We are a community resource committed to people who seek success in their families, careers and businesses. Our coordinated services promote personal responsibility, employability, continued education and financial stability." In 2000, the Center received a "tops in the nation" award from the U.S. Department of Labor and the American Association of Community Colleges for the comprehensive work in its One Stop process. The recognition came with a $10,000 award to be used to further the work at the Center.

The Newmark Center

Adjacent to the Newmark Center is the Family Center that provides classrooms and a laboratory for the College's Early Childhood Education and Family Studies program, campus daycare, drop-in childcare for the One-Stop Career Center, and childcare for JOBS participants. The Family Center not only provides counseling for parents, it provides a safe and controlled play environment for children. It was accredited by the National Association for the Education of the Young Child (NAEYC). The "Even Start" program provides funding for families with young children for early childhood education, and adult education for parenting as part of SWOCC's response to the needs of the community.

Again, SWOCC can be seen reaching out to the community it serves to provide not only the usual academic and vocational curricula but also help to those often left behind. As Kridelbaugh predicted, the Newmark Center and Family Center were able to pay for themselves through the partnerships with community stakeholders.

As for technology, during the 1990s considerable resources were directed toward keeping the campus up-to-date. The first step was the installation of a fiber optic network between buildings on campus, coupled with high bandwidth copper wire networks installed within each building. The number of computers available to students doubled on campus giving access to instructional software, e-mail and Internet services. Twelve classrooms were equipped with video projectors and sound systems linked to computers, VCRs and satellite downlinks. Ten smart boards were put to use that also interfaced with computers. The Computer Science (CS) instructional department at the College developed partnerships with Cisco Systems and Microsoft to enhance the teaching of state-of-the-art technology to their students.

The CS department grew and became a primary source for training in information technology on Oregon's South Coast. The department was selected in 2000 as one of only eight recipients in the nation for a $250,000 grant from Microsoft for the Working Connections project managed by the American Association of Community Colleges. During the first year of the grant, Microsoft also provided $900,000 worth of software to the College; in the second year, Microsoft added additional software valued at $780,000.[41]

According to Ms. Linda Kridelbaugh, vice president of Administrative Services, "We were the pilot for the pre-pathways program then called the "Career Ladder," which is now called "Pathways."

The campus culture in the '90s was different from the other decades as hundreds of students (including international students) from outside the College district made up a much higher percentage of the campus population than ever before. The

The Family Center

electronic distractions introduced to the nation in the 1980s both on and off the campus continued to influence the younger generation. Video games continued to be the rage. As one SWOCC professor put it, "The students could read, but they weren't in the habit of doing so."

As globalization and the world's environmental problems became pervasive and important, it became necessary for students and staff on campus to have a fundamental understanding of other cultures and people from around the globe. Dr. Kridelbaugh seized upon the opportunity to bring international education to SWOCC and in the early 1990s established sister-college relationships with Hyejeon Junior College in Choongnam-Do, Korea near Seoul and Changzhou Technical Institute in Changzhou, China.

In the early summer of 1992, Dr. Jong Kag Lee, an English instructor from Hyejeon (along with a few Korean students), came to SWOCC to teach conversational Korean and Korean culture and history on the SWOCC campus. As reported, Dr. Lee's course covered such topics as Korean art, music, folklore, language, literature, along with cultural thought and local lifestyles using video, audio tapes and film. Later that fall Orin Ormsbee, a local Coos Bay attorney, travelled to Hyejeon to teach conversational English to Korean students for two months. Asked how he liked the two month teaching assignment, Ormsbee stated: "If it were a permanent position, I would sell my law practice tomorrow!"

International students with their SWOCC degrees in 1998. Each year the International Student Club sponsored two great activities for the community and students: a cultural event and a food event highlighting the cultural and culinary aspects of their respective cultures.

The College welcomed students from both institutions to the campus in Coos Bay for periods of up to one year. It was the goal of the College to have between 30 and 50 international students attend SWOCC each year to promote international understanding. Over the past 20 years international students from more than 30 countries have attended SWOCC enriching the lives and educating staff, students, and the community at-large about their similarities and differences.

REDEFINING THE COLLEGE

The good news about the beginning of this decade was that the fears of Y2K did not materialize and the world continued working after the clock rolled over to January 1, 2000. However, the decade might be further characterized by the tragedy of 9/11 (September 11, 2001), George Bush[43], the Iraq and Afghanistan Wars, "don't ask; don't tell," cell phones, Internet, Kindle books, I-pads and I-phones, online shopping; Twitter, Facebook, and YouTube would dominate social media along with blogs and tweets and other strange acronyms that few understood; rising and falling stock prices, a housing bubble, bailouts and debacles, a deep recession, Hurricane Katrina and the Boxing Day Tsunami, Bernie Madoff and his Ponzie scheme, Michael Phelps and Barrack Obama.

It could also be said that trust in America reached one of its lowest levels not seen for many decades, if ever before. Some might even refer to the first ten years of the new century as the lost decade – only time will tell if this description sticks as historians desensitize the daily issues experienced during these ten years. Global warming came front and center for world politics and China shifted into high gear economically. The average minimum wage rose from $6 per hour in 2000 to $8.40 per hour as the decade closed.

The decade will also be remembered for Harry Potter books that were the rage among young and old alike. Reality television created open debates between those who loved it and those who did not. Near the end of the decade, gas prices soared above $4 per gallon as America once again came to the reality of its dependence on foreign oil and the British Petroleum oil rig disaster that caused untold damage to the Gulf of Mexico ecosystem. The Rover sent back spectacular pictures from Mars as its wheels left telltale tracks in the Martian soil. The Voyager space mission reached the outer limits of the Milky Way solar system with predictions that it will continue operating until 2020. The Genome Project would become 99% complete. And Captain Sully made history with his emergency landing of a commercial jetliner in the Hudson River with no loss of life.

SWOCC would face some of the most difficult financial challenges of its long history during the decade. After a decade of robust growth in the U.S. economy during the 1990s, and the meteoric growth in the tech industry leading up to the Y2K scare, two things happened to cause the decade to start out in a recession: 1) The bursting of the dot-com bubble by March 2000; and 2) The Federal Reserve's slowness to react by reducing interest rates at the nation's central bank. The Fed responded to the recession by lowering interest rates from 6.25% in December 2000 to 1.75% one year later, and the U.S. economy took off. Unfortunately, the speed and depth with which the interest rate reductions took hold caused the economy to overheat, especially in the housing markets. Mortgage lenders got very creative and potential home buyers leaped into the market with loans that were too good to be true!

In 2006, the Federal Reserve Bank began raising interest rates on overnight funds which in turn caused mortgage rates to climb and the sub-prime market to go "under water." In many instances the collateralized value of the homes that the banks carried on their books were well above the market value for the home, so bank foreclosures were inevitable. Fear gripped the financial industry as major institutions that had purchased packets of these "toxic mortgage assets" filed for bankruptcy and the federal government bailouts (Bear-Stearns, Fannie Mae/Freddie Mac, A.I.G., TARP, Citigroup, Bank of America, General Motors and Chrysler to name the major ones) took center stage during newscasts. By the fall of 2007, the financial industry in the United States was in great peril and the world in general was drawn into a free fall. This crisis became known as the Great Recession of 2007-2010.

How did this situation impact SWOCC? Remember the ballot measures discussed in an earlier chapter where financial support for schools was shifted from local property taxes to the State of Oregon's general fund? For the first half of the decade, the College found its State revenue sources first increasing then plummeting by decade's end, all while enrollment grew on campus and faculty salaries rose – albeit slightly from $9.044 million at the beginning of the decade to $12.666 million by decade's end. The State of Oregon faced a budget crisis as entitlement costs outpaced a shrinking tax base and the proportion of State funding to support SWOCC's rising enrollment fell from 51% (Community College Support Funds) of operating expenses at the beginning of the decade to 29% at the point where the College will officially graduate its 50th class in June 2011.

At the time this book was written in early 2011, the State of Oregon was facing a shortfall in balancing its budget by $3.5 billion. As the administration at the College looks to the 2011-2012 school year, they can expect further reduction in State funding by an amount likely in excess of $1.6 million. Other costs are also expected to increase. The cost of funding the College's Public Employees Retirement System will increase by $500,000 along with contractual increases of another $200,000. And the job of balancing the books at the College must rest squarely on the shoulders of its president as it moves forward into the next decade of life.

The financial crisis that gripped the nation at the end of the decade was further exacerbated by some serious mismanagement of the College's fiscal resources under President Judith Hansen's administration (2005-2008). As a result, Dr. Hansen left the College in a difficult financial condition. The community and the College were very fortunate to have Dr. Patty Scott on staff to step in as interim president in 2008 and make the difficult choices to bring the College budget back into balance. Unfortunately, for the College's financial health overall, Dr. Scott must continue to manage declining revenue sources from the State of Oregon while meeting the increasing demands of student enrollment and employee contracts. In her budget message to the Board of Education at the College for the 2009-2010 school year, Dr. Scott made the following introductory remarks:

> *"...This has been a very difficult budget to develop because of a variety of circumstances that have occurred internally over the past few years now converging with the State's economic crisis. State budget reductions created a need for additional staff reductions to lower our personnel costs along with extreme reductions to material and services to generate a balanced 2009-2010 budget. All three personnel groups, classified, faculty, and management suffered reductions. The College is functioning but we are extremely lean. During this challenging time to achieve a balanced budget, we made difficult decisions to do the least amount of harm while attempting to keep the core values of our educational system intact. We were pragmatic in making our decisions; always keeping in mind our vision and mission statements and the College strategic goals, while at the same time trying to move Southwestern Oregon Community College forward through the tough times..."*

In summary, the decade started out in a recession (2000-2001) and ended with a deeper one (2007-2010) with boom years (2004-2006) in between.

On a lighter note, let's take a brief look at some of the communication techniques used by the students on campus during the decade; the language of the 2000 decade: [35]

Newbie –	a newcomer
Rents –	parents
Brain fart –	forgetting something while talking
Senior moment –	forgetting something while talking

The list of slang words of this decade were much reduced from that of any previous time as talking was replaced by texting. Listed here are some of the texting abbreviations:

LOL –	laugh out loud
*$ –	I have a comment
10Q –	thank you
143 –	I love you
831 –	I love you
182 –	I hate you
2moro –	tomorrow
404 –	I haven't a clue
9 –	parents watching
99 –	parents not watching
B4N –	bye for now
BG –	be good
C-P –	sleepy
Def –	definitely
EMFBI –	excuse me for butting in
G2G –	got to go
KB –	kick butt
M4C –	meet for coffee
Ur –	you are
W8 –	wait
W9 –	wife in room
H9 –	husband in room
YY4U –	too wise for you

Etc. – and so it goes on and on with a new language! Will Webster redo his famous dictionary?

Texting in class became common as teachers struggled to capture the attention of students appearing to be taking notes, but who in reality were quietly communicating with their friends on portable electronic devices held in their lap and out of sight. A blind study conducted at a university in Pennsylvania indicated that 90% of the students texted while they were in class; 10% sent text messages

With help from the 2006-2011 Title III grant, 100% of the College classrooms are now multi-media or "smart" rooms supported by Integrated Technology Services.

during exams and 3% confessed to using texting to cheat on exams. The phenomenon is part of a new broader revolution in the way young adults communicate. Most prefer texting to e-mail and certainly to talking on the telephone. Some even indicated that texting was a right. Around 62% indicated that they should be allowed to text in class as long as it's not bothering other students; a challenge for parents footing the bill for post-secondary education.

Traffic police tried to find ways to stop the 'distracted driver' who was texting or talking on the cell phone while driving. The Oregon Legislature passed laws in 2008 with minor punishment for drivers caught with a cell phone to their ear or texting with one hand and steering with the other. Oprah Winfrey even launched a 'no phone zone' campaign encouraging celebrities and others to pledge not to talk or text while driving. Statisticians had fun comparing the reaction time of a driver on a cell phone and one who had consumed given quantities of alcohol. Apparently there are direct correlations!

Speaking of technology, the decade of 2000-2010 brought many improvements to SWOCC's technology in both instructional computing and administration. The College developed a large and varied technology infrastructure spanning the Coos Bay and Curry County campuses as well as three other off-site locations. For example, the College aquired a variety of technology-based methods to support instruction. With help from the 2006-2011 Title III grant, 100% of the College classrooms are now multi-media or "smart" rooms supported by Integrated Technology Services (ITS). By decade end, ITS supported three discrete Internet Protocol Video (IPV) classrooms, 23 student computer labs and 12 computer classrooms. ITS also coordinated live streaming media for academic and athletic events and IPV sessions for remote classes, as well as managing production of the Performing Arts Center events.

During the past five years, many improvements were added to the college-wide administrative software systems. The students had a full menu of financial, academic, and financial aid information along with online registration and degree audit. All advising faculty had access to a new advising module (e-Advising) which is fully online with interactive student communication functionality. The campus also had edge-to-edge wireless coverage allowing access to services from any location on both Coos and Curry campuses.

With a new College web page introduced in 2009, a content management system was rolled out so that all areas of the College would be able to keep their own content up to date, accurate and relevant. A web portal is currently being implemented and will be accessed from the College web site. Social networking is being integrated and academic and athletic events are now being streamed to the web. By decade end the College web site contained over 3,000 pages.

One can't help but marvel at the progress SWOCC has made to modernize their campus during the decade.

The previous two chapters of this book dealt rather extensively with the declining number of family-wage jobs in the College district and the growth of service oriented positions in big box stores or chain restaurants. Undaunted by these overwhelming economic challenges, in 2000, Dr. Kridelbaugh made it very clear that the College would play a role in helping to attract and retain family-wage jobs by doing all it could do to train an educated and versatile work force for the region:

> *"One of the goals of the College is to revitalize the economy and the workforce in this area. We do what we have to do to bring family-wage jobs into our area. If we don't have a trained workforce we cannot attract industry to move here."*

Putting people to work by expanding the College campus was one way SWOCC could add to the local economy. With a major gift to the SWOCC Foundation from Forrest and Marian Hales, the College began planning for the construction of a Performing Arts Center on campus. It was built for the benefit of the entire community, not just for campus students. The nearest performance center rivaling the Hales' project was 125 miles away in Eugene, Oregon.

Forrest and Marian Hales – 1995.

Forrest was a retired forester and land surveyor in Coos County and World War II veteran. He served on the College Foundation Board of Trustees and consistently supported the needs of the College. Marian was a homemaker and past 4-H leader who enjoyed the performing arts. She was a 50-year member of Beta Sigma Phi. Forrest and Marian began their investment in Southwestern Oregon Community College in 1994 by endowing a scholarship for graduates of the Coquille Valley High School. Later they made a significant contribution to the College's Family Resource Center and the Early Childhood Development program. Forrest and Marian passed away in 2005, but their legacy lives on at the Center and through their children (Susan Boal, Connie Gienger, and Bob Hales).

With the lead gift in hand, the College Board of Education authorized President Kridelbaugh to proceed with seeking funding to complete the project with an estimated cost of $4.4 million. In 2002, Mr. and Mrs. Hales established an

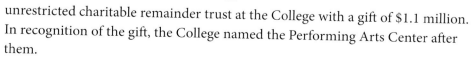

SOUTHWESTERN OREGON COMMUNITY COLLEGE
Performing Arts Center

An artist rendition of the Hales Center for the Performing Arts.

unrestricted charitable remainder trust at the College with a gift of $1.1 million. In recognition of the gift, the College named the Performing Arts Center after them.

Once again, the brush and forest had to be cleared away to make room for the new Performing Arts Center.

The stage area is pretty raw yet.

Dr. Kridelbaugh gives the College Board of Education a peek at the roughed out interior in the Hales Center for the Performing Arts.

The Hales Center for the Performing Arts is attached to Empire Hall. Along with the 12,000 square foot auditorium, the connection created a 2,000 square foot lobby useful for small celebrations and three small meeting rooms in Empire Hall that overlook the lake.

Here is what the performers on the stage would see at the Hales Center for the Performing Arts – without the 501 seats and an audience.

After 18 months of construction, the 501 seat Hales Center for the Performing Arts is ready to open – and once again, thanks go to Mr. and Mrs. Forrest Hales for their incredible generosity.

Dedication of the

HALES
Center for the Performing Arts

In memory of

Forrest John Hales
December 18, 1915 - March 17, 2005
and
Marian Luana Hales
February 16, 1920 - May 22, 2005

October 7, 2005

Next came the construction of the Oregon Coast Culinary Institute (OCCI) in 2005. According to Dr. Kridelbaugh, it all started when he and his wife Linda were having dinner at Gregson's Restaurant in North Bend, owned by Chef Robert Gregson. The chef had a habit of coming out of the kitchen to talk with the customers about their meals. He stopped at Kridelbaugh's table and their discussion turned to Gregson's background and his interest in starting a culinary institute at SWOCC. He mentioned that there were 170 culinary schools scattered throughout the United States with the best ones charging over $35,000 tuition. Gregson had seven years of teaching experience in a culinary institute in Miami, was an experienced star chef with credentials for teaching and could handle start up of a culinary program at SWOCC.

The discussion piqued Kridelbaugh's interest and when he returned to campus the next day, he asked his staff to do a survey of all the culinary institutes in the United States and find out about their curriculum and tuition. The SWOCC Foundation was asked to fund the survey, which was unanimously approved.

With a clear vision, but no real money to build another building on campus, the College cautiously started the Oregon Coast Culinary Institute in a building that had stood vacant for years. Previously known as the KC Steakhouse (east of and across the street from the Bi-Mart parking lot in North Bend), the College leased the building for $4,000 per month. The original program was two tiered – one-year programs led to a Certificate in Chef Training, while the two-year programs led to an Associate Degree in Applied Science in Culinary Arts Management (both programs being approved by the Oregon Department of Education). The goal that first year was to get 24 students enrolled in the program at a tuition rate of $12,000 per year. Since the beginning, 20 students have received a one-year certificate, 86 students have received an Associates degree in Culinary Arts and 31 students have received an Associates degree in Baking and Pastry.

Construction of the Oregon Coast Culinary Institute.

The demonstration kitchen at OCCI.

OCCI Class of 2009.

Once the concept/vision was proven, the College launched a construction program to build a state-of-the-art 15,000 square foot culinary teaching facility on the Coos Bay Campus at a cost of $3.5 million. Again, the College borrowed money through the sale of bonds to fund the project. Tuition paid by the ever increasing number of students at the Institute would retire the construction bonds, and the students would count toward the all consuming FTE formula. The majority of the students that enrolled at OCCI came from outside the district and generally utilized the newly constructed student housing.

Construction of the OCCI building started in 2005 following the approval of the architectural design submitted by Richard Turi. The Institute has three large teaching kitchens and three classrooms. There is also a large area for community banquets with beautiful open beam detailing and a state-of-the-art demonstration kitchen visible from the dining area.

On August 4, 2010, just five short years since construction of the Institute, a team from OCCI won a gold medal at the American Culinary Federation National Convention in Anaheim, California. Each team prepared a four-course meal and served it to 120 people. They were judged 100 percent on their technique, not just the quality of the food. [78]

The team will represent the United States in the youth category at the 2012 International Kochkunst Ausstellung/Culinary Olympics in Erfurt, Germany.

About the same time the OCCI building construction was getting underway, students on campus began to ask the College to provide a new recreational facility for students as well as space for the Associated Student Government, a student lounge, a second gym for intramural sports and a new athletic field. Prosper Hall was fully scheduled by the College's intercollegiate sports teams during the day and early evening, and the only time available for other students to use the gym for intramural activities was during the late evening hours.

The College began to explore the feasibility of building the new facility and determined that there were no third party revenue sources to pay for such a facility; if it were to be constructed, the revenue to amortize the debt would have to come through increased student fees. Upon determining by how much the fees would have to be increased, the College shared this information with the Associated Student Government; the students agreed that they wished to proceed and notified both the administration and Board of Education of their decision. Student input was sought and subsequently the facility was designed and approved by the students with the inclusion of a climbing wall and a room to hold dance instruction and other events. Much of the initial credit for this effort of keeping the students focused on the outcome and the cost of making it happen goes to Mr. Tom Nicholls, current executive director of Enrollment Management at the College. Construction of the facility was approved by the Board of Education and began in 2005.

While none of the SWOCC presidents were infatuated with having a football program on campus, a modern track and soccer field was constructed as part of the Recreation Center. Dr. Kridelbaugh continued to support the growth of the athletic programs at the College. Recruiting student-athletes was aggressively continued and today there are around 270 athletes participating in myriad intercollegiate competitions, with approximately 15% of them from within the College district boundaries. Asked how to bring the community more into the sports activity at the College, John Speasl said: "You need to have consistent winners. Otherwise, the community will question why spend the dollars on athletics that aren't winners? Therefore, we have to keep looking for the good kids to remain competitive; and we can't just do it with local kids. Winning helps with recruiting new athletes and hopefully gets the community behind the programs and not just the moms and dads."

Student Recreation Center built by Harmon Construction – 2005. The total cost of the 41,000 square foot Center was $4,962,000.

As we look back over the past 50 years, it is clear that Coos County has struggled to navigate the changes that impacted daily life in the region – especially during the past three decades. The current local economic situation reflects a long shift away from a production economy based upon wood products and fishing to a service economy with many franchised national companies. Family-wage jobs in the wood products industry have been replaced by lower-wage service jobs. Since 1976, jobs in lumber and wood products have declined by 82% in the region and with the loss of families in the communities, the number of children attending K-12 schools within the College district has dropped:

K-12 student enrollment Coos Bay, Myrtle Point and North Bend Districts

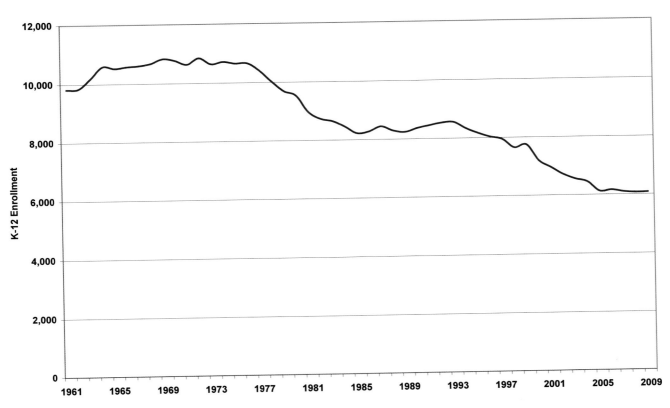

Here is shown the decline in the K-12 enrollments within the Coos Bay, North Bend and Myrtle Point School Districts. From this chart it is easily concluded that the future enroll- ment of students at SWOCC from within its district bound- aries will drop. In the past 10 years, the population of students in the K-12 schools within the entire College district has dropped by 30% from 13,500 in 1999 to 10,588 today.

Enrollment at SWOCC, on the other hand, has continued to grow, indicating the students are both recent high school graduates and adults seeking retraining. However, the percent of vocational courses vs. college transfer classes has reversed from what it was during the first 20 years of the College's existence. The College has grown in the direction of providing students an economical way to complete their first two years of college work. In 2010, SWOCC graduated 275 students with 307 degrees and/or certificates. [41]

145

As the decade unfolded, the distribution of students on the SWOCC campus changed:

	2000-01	2009-10
Full-Time	1,386	1,723
Part-Time	5,565	2,790
Average Age	39	25
Male	41%	43%
Female	52%	52%
Unknown	7%	5%
Traditional Aged (18-21)	752	1906
In-District	81%	80%
State Support	$6.444 million	$5.260 million
Federal Support	$0.089 million	$0.025 million
Local Support (taxes)	$3.411 million	$4.810 million
Tuition and fees	$1.423 million	$5.975 million

Increased environmental restrictions, technological advancements in production methods, government regulations and demographics changes all played a part in challenging the region's economy. Today, the largest age segment of the College district's population is 65 and older (21.2%); ages 50-59 second (15.8%); and 40-49 third (12.5%). Less than 20% have lived in the area for more than 10 years. [26]

Given the business cycles in the local economy, the change in the funding of schools in Oregon and the change in the social fabric comprising the population of the region, it is a remarkable achievement that Southwestern Oregon Community College has made over these past 50 years. Given the challenges of our nation, state and region, it has kept its head high and its boots moving forward. Today, classes are offered at the Coos Bay Campus, Curry Campus in Brookings, Gold Beach Center, Port Orford Center, and occasionally in other towns throughout the College district.

Even as the local economy ebbs and flows, graduates of the College contribute to the well being of their communities. Each year the College recognizes one alumnus, who is engaged in making their communities a better place, as a "Distinguished Alumni." The recipients of these awards are listed below:

1992 – Steve Greif – History teacher North Bend High School – *"I am proud of the fact that I've come back to the community from Southwestern and that I've made my contribution here."*

1993 – Mary Miller – Executive Director and CEO of the Oregon, Idaho, Montana Cystic Fibrosis Foundation – *"Southwestern has become a Miller family tradition."*

Steve Greif, Distinguished Alumnus, 1992

Peter Sorenson, Distinguished Alumnus, 1994

John Breuer, Distinguished Alumnus, 2002

1994 – Peter Sorenson – Eugene Attorney and Lane County Commissioner – *"I took a geography class and ended up getting a BA and MA in Geography because of the good start I got at Southwestern."*

1995 – Dr. Annette McGregor – Assistant Professor in the Theatre Division, Purdue University – *"I look back on my experiences at Southwestern as critical to my development as an artist, a teacher and a human being."*

1996 – Don Hall – CPA, Managing partner Yergen and Meyer, LLP (deceased) – *"The counselors and professors really care about the students and take a sincere interest in them. It really made a difference to me."*

1997 – Mark Nightingale – Engineer, Tektronix – *"Southwestern can prepare you for anything, because it's really the person, not the job. I encourage every student to follow his or her dream."*

1998 – Tsianina Means – 1997 ESPN Fitness America Champion, Miss Coos County 1993, Actress – *"I received a strong education, enjoyed the highly competitive athletic scene and made true lifelong friendships."*

1999 – Chuck Knight – Chief of Police, City of Coos Bay – *"The value of the College's program, whether it's criminal justice or any other program, is that it's well rounded and you get a good education."*

2000 - Peter Ruppe – Global Product Director, Nike, Inc. – *"The preparation at Southwestern really helped. The teachers were really outstanding and serious. They helped me focus and master what it took to do well in school."*

2001 – Michael Hennick, Sr. – Owner, Hennick's Home Center, Inc. – *"Southwestern allowed me to get a job in the forestry industry with skills that were directly applicable to the job."*

2002 – John D. Breuer – Physical Therapist, Southwest Physical Therapy, LLC. – *"Southwestern helped me refocus and become excited about college again. It is where my lifelong interest in science began."*

2003 – Robert "Gray" Jones – Poet and English Teacher, American International School of Vienna – *"A large portion of the credit for everything that happened to me at Southwestern I owe to the professors I met there. Coming to the College was like walking into a dream that just kept going once I left."*

2004 – Karl Kennedy – President and Chief Technical Officer, ORCA Communications – *"Some of my fondest Southwestern memories are of science and economics classes, and being on the wrestling team."*

2005 – Cynthia Ball – CFO/ Vice President of Administration at Coos Bay Lumber Company – *"At Southwestern, I received more than just an education. I learned how to set goals and then achieve those goals."*

2006 – Chuck McKay – President McKay's and Price 'N' Pride – *"I don't think there's an end to learning for any of us. My goal was not the credential or the diploma so much as the education and I certainly got that."*

2007 – Peggy Goergen – Retired Curry County Dean, SWOCC – *"Southwestern made it entirely possible for me to do what I wanted to do, which was to work in education. Even though I did not obtain a degree from Southwestern, I would not have been able to obtain a degree at all without Southwestern."*

2008 – Fran Worthen – Co-owner, Pacific Properties – *"There were so many things offered at the community college that just got you excited; all of them shape the fabric of a person's mind and emotions and they were all relevant. The community college opened doors for lifelong learning."*

2009 – Mary Stricker – Retired Library Director, SWOCC – *"Southwestern gave me confidence to continue my education which ultimately changed my life."*

2010 – Michael "Mick" Sneddon – Fire Chief, Charleston Rural Fire Protection District – *"My education from Southwestern has meant a world of knowledge and has opened doors, giving me the skills to seek what I need to excel."*

2011 – Linda Prefontaine – Western Region Sales for Pennington Crossarm Co. and Owner of Prefontaine Productions LLC

Chuck McKay, Distinguished Alumnus, 2006

Peggy Goergen, Distinguished Alumna, 2007

SWOCC's Curry County Campus
Pre-annexation

As with the beginning of Southwestern's Coos Bay Campus that started in the abandoned old Navy buildings in 1961, so was the story of developing college programs and eventually a SWOCC campus in Curry County.

In 1975, the Curry Education Service District began contracting with SWOCC for a county-wide Continuing Education Program. In 1978, funded by a CETA Title VI grant, the Adult Education Committee of Curry County launched a survey in Curry County to determine what educational opportunities were provided to the residents of Curry County and whether the County should form a separate Area Education District or continue to receive post-secondary education from SWOCC. Listed below were the major adult education resources within Curry County at the time of the survey:

1. Adult Basic Education (ABE) - This program was sponsored by the Coos-Curry Manpower Consortium in order to provide an opportunity for learning in five basic skill areas—mathematics, English, social science, natural science and literature. While the program was open to all, emphasis was placed on those without a high school diploma so they might qualify for a GED. It began operating around 1974. At the time, the program reached 85 people per year with no direct cost to the student. The format of instruction relied mainly on individual tutoring with classes given whenever two or more students were at the same level.

2. College of the Redwoods – Crescent City Branch - This program was sponsored by the College of the Redwoods. Its purpose was to provide the residents of northern coastal California and inadvertently the residents of southern coastal Oregon with Junior College level education. The cost to the student was $24 per unit with higher rates for non-residents.

3. Division of Continuing Education – Its purpose was to provide college level and post-graduate classes to persons who did not wish to enroll in a traditional college program. They were headquartered at SWOCC and around 45 students per year used the system from Curry County. The cost to the student was $25 per undergraduate credit hour and $40 for post graduate units.

4. Extension Service – This program was sponsored by Oregon State University. In 1977, there were 193 participants in the Extension's short courses. The courses were usually free and around 15 programs were offered annually.

5. Humbug Mountain Committee – The Humbug Mountain Committee (HMC) was established to stimulate, promote and develop interest in the arts, crafts, sciences and humanities. It used facilities provided by libraries and schools. In 1977, this program served 4,000 people. HMC offered about 20 programs per year.

6. Open Enrollment in High School – This program was sponsored by the K-12 school districts in which a high school was located and provided adults the opportunity to participate in programs offered at the school.

7. Pelican Bay Arts Association – This program provided instructional opportunities to the public in the field of art. The program was staffed by volunteers and was self supporting.

8. Port Orford Adult Education Committee – This committee was sponsored by the 2CJ School District. Its purpose was to meet the post-secondary educational needs of the school district residents – including vocational, basic skill and interest classes. It also assisted SWOCC with their outreach programs.

9. State Apprentice Program – This program was sponsored by the Oregon State Bureau of Labor and its purpose was to enable people to become qualified craft workers in various fields.

10. SWOCC Outreach – This program was sponsored jointly by SWOCC and the Curry County Intermediate Education District. Its purpose was to provide education beyond the high school level to the general public. Through coordination with the Coos Curry Education Service District, SWOCC provided post-secondary education courses since 1975. They offered coursework in various classrooms throughout Curry County. The program served about 1,000 in 1977 and the College was allocated 50 FTE for that year. Advisory committees, such as the Port Orford Education Committee, in each location helped to plan and implement various community education offerings, including non-credit enrichment courses. [87]

11. Other Programs – Humboldt State University Extension, Community Action and the Curry County Hospital.

After six meetings, the Committee concluded that the time was not right to launch an effort to form a new educational based taxing district and the minutes show that there was "no apparent threat that SWOCC would forcibly annex Curry County." Educational programs continued on a status quo basis for another decade with most efforts gradually consolidating under the Adult Education Coordinator hired at Curry ESD. Curry ESD and SWOCC gained funding for this program through a state pool of "Contracted Out of District" funds set up by the State Legislature. Initially, the funding included all undergraduate and life enrichment courses, but the funding guidelines gradually began being cut back to a more collegiate program.

In January 1988, a petition was filed by the citizens of Curry County with the State Board of Education to form a Community College Service District within the County; 504 valid signatures were submitted. Some of the underlying effort rested with the desire to bring a new Business Development Coordinator from the State Employment Division to the area in an effort to increase employment in the region. To qualify for the placement of an employee from the agency, one of two actions was required: either the region was part of a community college district or it had to be a community college service district. (It might be prudent here to describe the difference between a community college district and a community college service district. The former is locally controlled and locally governed. It is concerned with providing lower division college work, vocational preparation, Adult Basic Education, and general education courses to the population at-large.

It may also own buildings and property. A "community college service district" may not purchase property; it may rent space in other facilities and contract for instructors from other qualified institutions. It could employ teachers and staff to provide certain programs. The service district allows the region to collect the resources within the area to maximize the breadth of educational offerings.) As required by statute, the following five issues had to be addressed before the State Board would authorize a new service district:

- Educational needs of the area

- Potential enrollment levels

- Size and duration of a serial levy or size of a tax base required to meet the local share of operating and capital expenses

- Relationship of proposed district to the overall plan for all education in the State

- Boundaries of the proposed district

A consultant, Robert C. Kelly, was hired to address each of the above issues. The major conclusions reached by the consultant were very similar to the arguments posed by Henry Hansen in his quest to form a college district 30 years earlier:

1. *A significant demand and need for community college services exists within Curry County.*

2. *This demand and need are not being met by the current levels of available services.*

3. *The proposed Curry County Community College Service District appears to have the potential to double the number of equivalent full-time students within the first four years of operation.*

4. *The demographic isolation of Curry County amplifies the difficulty of its citizens to obtain post-secondary education.*

5. *A three-year serial levy not to exceed $.22 per thousand of assessed valuation would provide an adequate local share of funding to meet the initial operating expenses of the district.*

6. *The formation of a Curry County Community College Service District would serve the overall plan for education in the State of Oregon.*

7. *The boundaries of the proposed district, as including all of Curry County, are clear and reasonable.*

In hindsight, one must wonder how such positive projections could have been made as the entire southern coast of Oregon remained in the economic doldrums. The State Board of Education turned down their application. Immediately, the Adult Education Director at the time, Judy Stringham, vowed to change the outcome the next time around and hired Janet Pretti to increase class offerings and college awareness in the northern part of the county. Meanwhile, Brookings

Harbor School District 17-C, in a budget crunch, cut the long time position of Adult Education Coordinator, and deferred all local adult offerings to the ESD. Peggy Goergen, who had held that position, moved to the ESD as an assistant to Stringham and eventually took over the director position when Stringham left to pursue other goals. In the process of trying to obtain more help from the State, educators and local citizens in the region reached out to other community colleges to determine their interest in annexing Curry County to their boundary – Rogue Community College and Umpqua Community College were approached and again the Oregon State Board of Education told the residents that they belonged as part of SWOCC.

As mentioned earlier, when Ballot Measure 5 was passed by Oregon voters, it capped the property taxes dedicated for school funding at $15 per $1,000 of real market value per year, gradually lowering the cap to $5 over a five-year period. Funding for local schools shifted from primarily local property tax funds to State funds as the State backfilled the lost property tax allocation for K-12 schools through an equalization formula based on the number of students in each district. By 1995, 98% of Curry taxpayers were paying the $5 cap for their local K-12 schools.

Annexation into the College District

Just as Henry Hansen is given credit for making the SWOCC district a reality in Coos County, Mr. Larry Minnich's advocacy was critical to the 1995 successful campaign to annex Curry County into the College district. In the early 1990s, Rural Development Initiatives had assembled community response teams in Curry's three incorporated cities to envision their communities in 2010. Independently, all three groups concluded that expanded collegiate offerings and Small Business Development Center services were needed to create opportunity for their residents and businesses. Larry Minnich was a member of the Gold Beach 2010 Committee. When he realized that other parts of the State were getting K-12 and community college services for the same $5 cap that Curry County residents paid, he was convinced that joining the College district was essential.

Larry Minnich receiving the Volunteer of the Year award as presented by the Oregon Community Education Association for his leadership and dedication to bringing Curry County into the SWOCC district.

By this time, the Small Business Development Centers had become part of the Community College system. A further incentive to the motivation in Curry County was the reality of these services being unavailable unless a given area was part of a community college district. The COD (Contracted Out of District) system was also being revamped (and was eventually eliminated), which meant that the funding pool could disappear and FTE (Full Time Equivalency) funding would only come to community colleges.

Minnich just had to figure out a way to explain the nuances of Ballot Measure 5 so that Curry voters would understand that they could vote for the community college without raising their taxes. Like Hansen, he worked tirelessly on the ensuing grassroots campaign to make it happen, traveling frequently with Dr. Kridelbaugh to Salem to testify before the Legislature on behalf of the College and extending services to Curry County. Current SWOCC Board member Cherie Mitchell remembers collecting petition signatures, staffing phone banks and information booths, distributing yard signs, collecting donations for newspaper ads, and doing anything and everything to get the word out on the benefits of a community college before the vote.

When the question of annexation went to a vote in 1995, Curry County voted to join the Southwestern Oregon Community College District. As a result there were three positive outcomes for Curry County residents:

1. K-12 funding remained the same;

2. Southwestern began receiving property taxes to provide services in Curry County; and

3. More than 98% of taxpayers in Curry County did not pay additional property taxes to become a part of the Southwestern District and receive expanded college services.

Gold Beach Center – 2010

The other win for the annexation was the fact that the College now had the opportunity for significantly more FTE reimbursement funds from the State as the focus of the Curry Program moved from primarily a community education program to providing more post-secondary education.

The first task following annexation was to transition the existing Curry Adult Education Program from a Curry ESD contracted program with SWOCC to a full-fledged part of SWOCC. The partnership had been in existence since 1975, with classes, staff and offices in place. The Curry Education Service District Program was based in Gold Beach, with satellite offices at Brookings-Harbor High School (in the former ticket booth) and in Port Orford in a shared office space with a SCBEC Home Health program. The ESD staff consisted of Peggy Goergen, director of Adult Education, and two part-time staff. Goergen was appointed to interim associate dean status at the College, the part-time staff moved into full-time positions, and three additional part-time staff members were hired. One of the new hires was Jim Bouley. As the Curry Small Business Development Center (SBDC) coordinator, he delivered the long coveted SBDC's free counseling and business workshops until his untimely death in November 2008.

Port Orford Center – 2010

Because research showed that a branch campus is more successful when based in the area's population center, Dr. Kridelbaugh immediately moved to establish the home base for SWOCC's Curry addition in Brookings, and to find a new home for the Gold Beach Center independent of the Curry Education Service District. Temporarily, the Brookings Center opened fall of 1995 in a storefront and for the price of a "donation," the Gold Beach High School wrestling team was "hired" to move the Gold Beach Center to the Curry County Fairgrounds. Even the Port Orford office was uprooted several times in the early years before settling into a partnership with the North Curry Service Integration Center, a tiny version of the one stop service model that led to the creation of the Newmark Center on the Coos Bay Campus.

The Brookings Campus was originally housed in the vacated local library building. Immediately before the College acquired the facility, it was used for a short time as a community thrift store ca. 1997. Pictured: back row, Peggy Goergen; front row L. to R., Kathleen Michelson, Carol Imada, Mary Whitaker, and Janet Pretti.

In 1997, the Brookings Center moved into the newly refurbished former Chetco Library, at 420 Alder Street as a tenant, and purchased it two years later to avoid becoming homeless when it was put up for sale. The staff and students were thrilled to have three separate classrooms and a state-of-the-art computer lab with full Internet access for instruction. Two full-time faculty members were hired, in English and computer science. To meet the requirements of the Conditional Use Permit to use the facility for educational purposes, the College had to expand parking from the two spaces that came with the building. The Christian Science Reading Room across the street generously agreed to share its parking lot with the College and the USFS let the College develop an adjacent vacant lot into a parking lot. [89] In 2008, the College purchased the USFS parking lot in order to retain the parking spaces required for the Conditional Use Permit. Community buildings, schools, churches, and business continued to be used throughout the County for classes and events. Science classes were only taught in the evenings when high schools labs were available.

Growing the Program

In the 1994/95 academic year, the local Curry classes generated 110.691 FTE, including lower division (transfer) classes and community education. Collegiate programs grew steadily, finally surpassing community education offerings in 2002/03. In the 2009/10 academic year, local Curry classes generated 186.761 FTE. Online classes were introduced in the early 2000s but did not start being tracked separately until 2003/04. That year online classes taken by Curry residents generated 8 FTE; by 2009/10 it had grown to 24 FTE. The availability of online classes has been essential for most Curry students, giving them a wider option of courses and programs than would be possible locally.

In the 1994/95 academic year, one Port Orford resident earned an AAS in Manufacturing Technology on the Coos Bay campus and one Brookings resident earned a certificate in bookkeeping through classes on the Curry Campus. In the 2009/10 academic year, 23 Curry residents earned 25 degrees and certificates from Southwestern - 16 transfer degrees (AAOT, ASOT and AS), seven AAS degrees (including three nursing graduates from the Curry cohort) and two certificates. All in all, 126 Curry residents have earned 143 degrees and certificates in the first fifteen years Curry County has been part of the College district - 73 transfer degrees, 39 AAS degrees, four AGS degrees, and 27 certificates. Four Southwestern valedictorians have lived and earned their degrees in Curry County: Rebecca Hoft (1999), Susan Brady (2005), Arnold Sylvester (2010), and Rebecca Chierichetti (2011).

The first South Coast Writers Conference was held in Gold Beach in 1995. Bob Simons, a local retiree, had expressed his dream of a local writers' conference to Ms. Goergen for years. With the upcoming vote on annexation, Goergen decided it was a good time to get some publicity for the College. Simons' vision was to create a high quality, affordable conference in the off-season when the local economy needed a boost. The conference has been held every year since, attracting an average attendance of about 100 in recent years. The reputation of the conference has steadily grown with potential presenters as well, attracting northwest authors with national reputations.

The arrival of the Southwestern University Center in 1998, three years after Curry's annexation, was timely for the growing numbers of college bound students. Curry's first University Center graduate earned a bachelor's degree in 2001. As of 2010, Curry students had earned 22 bachelor's and four master's degrees through SWOCC's University programs while continuing to live and work on the South Coast.

Joining the College district also made possible a new level of collaboration with local high schools. Southwestern awarded two full tuition scholarships to each in-district high school and Curry high schools immediately qualified. In 1999/2000, a new statewide program reached Curry County allowing high school students to earn college credits while still in high school, as long as their instructor was qualified to teach at the community college level and the course was taught to college standards. Pacific High School was the only Curry high school that participated that first year – two classes were articulated, 14 students earned credits, and 53 college credits were earned. Originally students were charged 10% of the tuition as a transcription fee, but beginning in 2005/06, the credits were free to students. In 2009/10, all three Curry high schools participated – 21 classes were articulated, 143 students earned credit and 991 college credits were earned. Peggy Goergen retired in 2007. Jason Wood served as the Curry dean from July 2007 to October 2008, at which time Janet Pretti was promoted from Curry program coordinator to dean (first as an interim, then as dean in 2009).

Building for the Future – The New Curry Campus

The Brookings Center on Alder Street was never intended to be a long-term home for the College's Curry operations. President Kridelbaugh had started a building fund by setting aside $500,000 in each of the first two years that Curry County was admitted to the district. The search for a site and for additional funding began in earnest once the Brookings Center was settled into the Alder Street facility.

In 2001, State Senator Ken Messerle and Representative Wayne Krieger secured $960,000 in State funds for construction of the Curry facility. This, combined with the $1 million set aside by Kridelbaugh, seemed like enough money at the time to build a new campus – if somehow land would be donated to the College within the City of Brookings with the entire infrastructure already in place. But property sales were booming in the late '90s and early 2000s, so no land donations were forthcoming, and every property suitable for the project had a price tag of $1 to $2 million, leaving little funds for construction of a building.

Dr. Patty Scott is seen here receiving the deed from Rio Tinto Minerals executive Dennis Boyle.

The most promising early prospect was collaboration with Oregon Parks and Recreation Department and Brookings Harbor School District. The Oregon Parks had acquired the Crissey Field, a forty acre site close to California, and was planning to relocate the Harris Beach Visitor Center. Brookings-Harbor High School was looking for a way to relieve its overcrowding and the College needed a campus. Paul Prevenas, Brookings Harbor School District superintendent, approached the College and Oregon Parks about developing the existing visitor center site on the east side of Highway 101 for a new high school / college facility. Preliminary plans were drawn up, but opposition to moving the high school scuttled the plan.

In 2001, the College began a conversation with U.S. Borax (acquired later by Rio Tinto Minerals – a Brazilian company) about including the College in their proposed Lone Ranch development project north of Brookings. Borax had owned the property for over 100 years. In the 1960s, when Highway 101 was being upgraded, Borax gave a portion of this holding west of the highway for a state park with the caveat that for this gift, the State would allow five access points to the highway from the company's property to the east. In addition, the entire Borax property was later included in the Brookings Urban Growth Boundary which would facilitate the permitting process to develop their land to the extent they wanted. Shortly thereafter, U.S. Borax submitted its master plan to the City of Brookings for approval of its 600+ home subdivision to be completed in multiple phases. It included a designated 10-acre site for the future SWOCC Curry Campus. The master plan was approved October 11, 2004.

In March 2007, U.S. Borax signed an agreement to donate ten acres of land at their Lone Ranch site to SWOCC upon final approval of the College's detailed development plan. After several challenges by local citizens to the College's development, the City of Brookings approved the plans on September 1, 2009, allowing the College to begin the final steps of transferring title of the ten acres of land to the College. U.S. Borax and College officials celebrated the transfer with the community on February 4, 2010. The gift of land was valued at $1,750,000. At the event, Dr. Scott commented, "It took nine years to get the land, and we have only 18 months to move in. Things will move very quickly."

Why the rush? In 2005, Representative Krieger and Senator Messerle had been successful in including $2.3 million of capital construction matching funds for a Curry Campus; it was the first capital construction appropriation for community colleges since 1989. However, the $2.3 million from the State had to be matched by an identical local amount and the State's money had to be spent by June 30, 2011.

Several things had changed in the intervening nine years. Even though the property was located within the Brookings Urban Growth Boundary, the property had no water, sewer service or adequate power for the subdivision or the campus. Originally, the first phase of the Lone Ranch development and the Curry Campus were scheduled to begin simultaneously with the Borax development and the College sharing the costs of infrastructure development. With the State money match deadline looming, and the Tio Tinto Minerals project delayed, the College had to proceed alone, adding about $2 million for infrastructure costs to the project.

The entrance road to the site for the new Curry Campus.

Compounding the problem was the fact that the College's fiscal crisis of 2008 had absorbed the cash reserves intended for the Curry project. A fundraising campaign was launched and plans were made to fund the project in the same way the College had funded previous projects – through the sale of bonds. But the national banking and bond crisis of 2008 had brought regulation changes to how bond ratings were determined. For the first time the College would have to go out on the open market and earn a bond rating. The College was between a rock and a hard place. It needed more money than expected and it was going out for a bond rating only 18 months after the College had begun confronting its own financial crisis – and in a climate where every bond rating was being carefully scrutinized by regulators.

There was one ray of light that came from a surprising source – in an effort to stimulate the economy, the American Recovery and Reinvestment Act (ARRA) passed by Congress in February 2009 had created a new type of bond – Recovery Zone Economic Development bonds (RZED). Those bonds were for shovel ready projects, and in return for embarking on capital improvement projects in precarious times, the federal government would pay 45% of the interest for the life of the bond. Oregon had distributed its allocation in varying amounts to individual counties for projects to be determined locally. When it became apparent that neither Coos nor Curry Counties were planning to use their allocation, the College asked each to recommend to the State that SWOCC be allowed to use their share. They did, and in the end the College received additional unused allocations increasing SWOCC's RZED bond allocation to $6.115 million.

On April 27, 2010, the SWOCC Board of Education demonstrated its continued confidence in the vision of the College to provide educational opportunities for students by unanimously adopting a resolution to finance the costs of constructing the new Curry County Campus in Brookings. The total cost of the construction will be $8.3 million, which will provide 26,800 square feet of space under a single roof. On June 16, 2010, Dr. Scott signed the contract with Ausland Builders, Inc. for construction of the campus. On the same day, SWOCC sold the bonds to fund the project on the open market. The College had earned an "A" rating from Standard & Poor's, a clear recognition that the previous 18 months of budget cuts and layoffs had resulted in a return of the College finances to stable ground – much of the credit for this effort goes to President Patty Scott and her administrative staff. Because the College had earned the A rating, it was able to issue debt at an effective interest rate of 3.366% and saved the College an estimated $536,000 in debt service payments.

The Curry Campus facility is also being designed as a community hub for short-term training and conferences. The community wing can be used for college classes, but can easily transition into a conference area. Its two large rooms can each be divided into two smaller rooms. It also offers an after-hours entrance/reception area and access to a catering/demonstration kitchen. Larger events can utilize the nearby two-story commons area. The commu-

A group of donors and staff tour the building 'in-progress' – June 2011.

nity wing will provide a new and sorely needed venue for large public and private gatherings in Curry County. It is being designed so that the regular work of the College can continue with minimal disruption when it is in use for those events. The Grand Opening of the Curry Campus is planned for January 27, 2012.

The new Curry Campus will be a two-story building equipped with wireless Internet and all the features needed for 21st century learning. There will be seven independent classrooms including an allied health suite supporting expanded nursing, basic nursing assistant training, medical assistant and EMT training, a science lab, a computer lab and classrooms with SMART technology and IPV (Internet Protocol Videoconferencing) connectivity. Photo courtesy of Janet Pretti.

The SWOCC Foundation

Throughout the 50 year history of the College, a partnership existed that provided private funds to assist with special projects and scholarships for students. On January 1, 1962, eight months after the College district vote was affirmed, the Southwestern Oregon Community College Foundation was incorporated as a private 501(c)(3) organization. Its main purpose is to receive contributions from individuals and organizations in order to establish endowments to fund specific activities at the College – mainly scholarships. Even in those beginning years, students who needed financial aid were awarded scholarships by the SWOC (sic) Board of Education.

SWOCC Foundation Scholarship winner from Brookings Harbor High School, Trinity DeHasler.

According to Dr. Kridelbaugh, in the early years, the Foundation was used as a clearinghouse for scholarship contributions given to the College by individuals or organizations. There appeared to be limited efforts put forth to solicit funds from the community at-large until the early 1990s, when it became part of the administration's strategies of funding the growth of the College. Today, the Foundation is actively involved in fundraising for worthy college programs – particularly student scholarships and assisting with the funding of capital projects. As Karen Pringle, the current executive director of the Foundation, said, "Expanding and broadening the cultural and educational life of the south coast through Southwestern is the most worthwhile pursuit I can imagine." The vision of the Foundation is to pursue "fund raising and friend raising" for the College.

The scholarship program at SWOCC was launched in 1961 with a gift of $200 from the local Kiwanis Club. Dr. Van Loan wanted to encourage students to get involved in student government. As such, a year after taking over the leadership at the College, he recommended to the Board that scholarships be given to those students inclined to take a leadership role in student body affairs.

The Board of Education minutes of August 12, 1963 record information from Dr. Van Loan:

> *"We are continually getting loan money and also many outright scholarships. Board members are pleased with the amount of money being received for the people who may need financial help. Dr. Van Loan reported that every critical emergency case for student financial assistance that the school is aware of has been taken care of."*

Today, the Foundation manages a portfolio of about $3.0 million in liquid assets that it utilizes to accomplish its mission of supporting students and the campus at-large. Along with it's executive director, the Foundation is guided by a voluntary Board of Trustees.

The best way to understand the meaning of the scholarships awarded by the SWOCC Foundation is to read some of the "thank-yous" that were handwritten by the students who received them. A young woman by the name of Valerie wrote the following back in 1995:

> "I came to SWOCC very afraid and uncertain of my ability to earn a college education and what I found was more encouragement, support and help than I ever thought possible. My experience at SWOCC has been so positive – everyone from my instructors, advisors and counselors to the administrative staff has taken an interest in helping me achieve my goals. Thanks especially to those of you involved in making scholarships available to students such as myself. Thank you for the gift of an education."

The SWOCC Foundation and the College joined resources on June 15, 2007 to form the Laker Club Alumni Association. In the inaugural year of the Laker Club, 580 Southwestern alumni joined as charter members. The Laker Club was organized to build a stronger allegiance between SWOCC and its graduates. Membership in the Association is free; members receive e-mail newsletters, invitations to various Laker Club events each year, and the opportunity to connect and network with other former Southwestern students. The Club is open to anyone who has taken a class at Southwestern. In the spring of 2010, the membership of the Laker Club stood at 820 members.

One of the facts often overlooked in writing about the history of people, places and things is the softer side of the topic. In this case, it is the artwork that is sprinkled about the College campus, enhancing the natural beauty of the College. The SWOCC Foundation helps sponsor a program called Visions in concert with the local Coos Art Museum. The juried competition is open to high school art students throughout southwestern Oregon. The event helps to promote the arts with financial awards and two-year tuition waivers granted to the three top artists. The winning pieces are added to the Foundation's permanent collection and are displayed in the Hales Center for the Performing Arts and in various offices throughout campus.

Although recently discontinued, in the past the Southwestern Foundation also supported the expansion of the campus' permanent art collection by partnering with the Coos Art Museum to sponsor the Expressions West art exhibits and competitions. Expressions West was also a juried exhibition featuring works chosen from hundreds of submissions made by professional and amateur artists from many western states. The top three pieces of art were acquired by the Foundation and currently hang in the lobby of the Hales Center for the Performing Arts, the Oregon Coast Culinary Institute and other buildings on the campus.

*Visions 2004 – First Place,
Monica Johnson – Portrait*

Dr. Kridelbaugh had a vision of bringing art onto campus to add cultural diversity and attract visitors to the area. As a result the Board of Education commissioned several sculpture pieces that can be found throughout campus.

Expressions West – First Place 2005,
Kimberly Wursler – Early Birds

Expressions West – Second Place 2002,
Mary Cenyar – The Salmon Fisherman/Feed the People

Expressions West – Second Place 2004,
Gary Everest – The Old Teapot

Expressions West – Third Place 2001,
Cora Larson – Port Orford

In the winter of 2000, the College commissioned local artist Mack Holman to create two bronze sculptures for a permanent display on campus. Part of the agreement was that Holman teach students how to make bronze sculptures. Holman mentioned how surprised he was by the variety of students enrolled in his class – there was a professional artist and a dentist working side by side. Some students had 30 or more years of welding while others had no experience at all. According to Holman, the students did most of the work on the sculpture. "…They did most of the pourings, the grinding and fitting the pieces together. The students welded 22 different pieces to create the sculpture…"

Between Classes, Mack Holman, 2000

Art, theatre, academics, vocational and athletic programs at the College would not happen without the amazing partnerships, grants and collaborations that have occurred over the years. These partnerships were with both private and public entities. The reader is directed to the Appendix for a more complete sampling of these relationships.

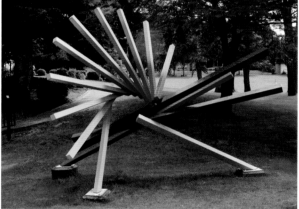

Above: Sundance, Roslyn Mazzilli, 2003
Below: Wind, Carol Gold, 1999

Liberation, Phillip Levine, 1998

As we approach the 50th year of operations at the College, it is important to understand the future direction the administration and Board foresee. In 2010, the Board of Education at SWOCC adopted the following vision and mission statements along with the core values for the College:

VISION STATEMENT
Southwestern leads and inspires lifelong learning.

MISSION STATEMENT
Southwestern Oregon Community College serves the educational and cultural needs of our students and communities by providing access to quality education in a professional and engaging environment which supports innovation, sustainability and lifelong enrichment. Learning experiences are characterized by excellent teaching, support for student achievement and the enhancement of social and economic opportunities.

CORE VALUES
Community – Build collegiality by providing a welcoming and supportive atmosphere with respect for diversity.
Learning – Filter every decision, activity, and function through the lens of learning.
Innovation – Empower creative, progressive thinking that results in a sustainable, positive change.
Professionalism – Present ourselves with honesty and integrity working together to achieve our goals.
Stewardship – Sustainably manage our environment and fiscal resources to support our staff, students, and community.

CORE THEMES with ASSOCIATED STRATEGIC PLAN GOALS
Access – Access is the pathway to learning opportunities for students and the community members through support services and diverse delivery methods.
1. Ensure access to diverse learning opportunities.
2. Provide access to support services for students, staff, and the community.

Learning and Achievement – Student learning and student achievement are at the core of the College mission by emphasizing quality teaching; quality learning; quality course and program design; retention; persistence; completion; graduation and/or transfer.
3. Maintain and develop quality learning opportunities to encourage student success and achievement.
4. Support student lifelong learning and attainment of goals.

Innovation and Sustainability – Innovation and sustainability are interwoven by seizing opportunities for resource development by means of entrepreneurism, grant development, and the College Foundation that support the maintenance of a strong infrastructure of employees, technologies, facilities, resource management, and educational programs through the continual improvement process.
5. Create the vision and structure for long-term college sustainability and growth.
6. Support college growth through planning, budgeting, and assessment.
7. Allocate resources to support continuous improvement for a strong infrastructure of employees, technologies, facilities, and educational programs.

Community Engagement – Community engagement is the means to build strong partnerships and provides opportunities for the community to participate in diverse activities and events.
8. Sustain and build strong community, business, and agency partnerships.
9. Promote and provide opportunities for the community to engage in diverse activities and events.

Approved April 26, 2010 • Effective July 1, 2010

Since 1961, a group of 61 men and women have volunteered their time, talents and energy to the Board of Education to help steer the College and meet the vision of providing exceptional educational opportunities to the people of southwestern Oregon.

Obviously the president of any organization plays a vital role in creating a vision and is tasked with "setting the table" for the future. The president's staff, advisors and boards weigh in at appropriate times to assist and approve the process and the results. When asked about her goals for the College in the future, President Patty Scott, made the following observations:

> *"I would like the communities within the College district to think of us as a resource for whatever issues they may have. I want them to get to know us and to use the resources of the College. I would also like to see the University Center grow in such a way that more four-year bachelor's programs are offered without the local students having to leave the SWOCC campus to get their degrees. I do not want to create a four-year college, but simply to provide a conduit where rural students can get advanced degrees at a more affordable cost. I would like to see us use our own faculty to instruct upper-division courses; we have qualified faculty with PhD's who could teach these classes. There should be more seamless course teachings whether it is at the university or at the community college levels. After all, it's all about the student's education and lifelong learning – isn't it?"*

Today as we look out into the future of education in Oregon, and for that matter across the United States in total, four issues remain in the forefront of education:

1.   THE FTE – The continual pursuit of the number of students attending the institution – the Full-Time Equivalent – the State's financial reimbursement formula. Today, Oregon has created a system where the FTE state reimbursement is proportionate to the number of students, and therefore the growth in enrollment at community colleges in the urban communities is disproportionately higher than in the rural regions. Why? Because that is also where the number of unemployed is the highest - maybe not proportionately, but in pure numbers returning to college for retraining. Unless something changes in the allocation of FTE dollars from the State, the urban/rural competition for funds will become greater.

2.   THE UNDERPREPARED STUDENTS – There remains a disturbing trend as demonstrated by new students who took the COMPASS placement test. There were years at SWOCC where 92% of these new students were not ready to undertake college level courses – particularly math and English. While the colleges will continue to do all they can through developmental courses, this problem is systemic across the country. From home life, to K-12 learning, to society's needs in general, the problem is widespread. [89]

3.   ONLINE EDUCATION – The world at-large has become more and more comfortable with taking education courses online via the Internet, and the capability of those courses to mimic face-to-face learning with a professor continues to improve. Will online classes displace the traditional campus of bricks and mortar? Only time will tell, but unquestionably, SWOCC must continue to change to meet those needs in order to stay competitive. Since education has become somewhat of a commodity, the College must find those areas where it can have and maintain a competitive advantage over other institutions of higher learning by providing a " suite of e-services" to meet a broader need of the online students. Access to education is no longer restricted by geography.

4.   THE COST OF EDUCATION – One can easily expand this topic beyond the post-secondary level of education to include all levels of education in general. However, and as we have seen referenced throughout this book, SWOCC has a cost advantage over the four-year colleges, but it also must provide for the original tenets of its creation – provide for transfer courses, vocational courses and general adult education programs – something the four-year colleges are not required to do. There are seventeen community colleges scattered throughout Oregon that are all essentially providing the same type of courses and are all competing for similar dollars.

The big question then remains – How will Southwestern Oregon Community College differentiate itself from its competion in the future? In the end, as it is today, it will be about the success of their graduates.

Today, Tioga Hall, or as it was originally called – The Learning Resource Center – stands as the College sentinel proudly overlooking its domain of the beautiful Coos Bay Campus at Empire Lakes. Photo ca 1970.

Someday, someone will write another story about this little college in southwestern Oregon that started with 815 students in ramshackle buildings scattered throughout the County. Tuition and fees amounted to $65 per term in that first year. Today there are around 10,000 students enrolled on campus. With tuition of $69 per credit hour plus an additional $17 per credit hour for course fees, the total cost for a full-time student taking 12 credit hours per term is approximately $1,100 per term. The future story of SWOCC will undoubtedly seize upon that distant vision by a few to form a community college to improve the future opportunities for the children of the region.

Henry Hansen would be proud to know that over the past 50 years, more than 100,000 full-time students have attended SWOCC with thousands more taking classes simply to better their lives. Over the past 20 years alone, over 55,000 FTE have been credited to the College by the State.

A beautiful campus rose from swampland surrounding a lake into a modern community college – a proud community investment for sure. One only needs to stand in the center of campus and look at the buildings, the sculptures, the landscape and the eager eyes of the students to realize just how valuable this asset is to our area. The community wishes them good sailing as they leave the harbor for the next 50 years.

SOUTHWESTERN OREGON COMMUNITY COLLEGE
BOARD OF EDUCATION MEMBERS

ORVILLE ADAMS 1961–1966	MERLEN FREEMAN 1965–1977	DR. AMELIA LIPTON QUINN 1971–1975	RUSSELL HALL 1978–1981	KAY HEIKKILA 1985–1988	DAN SMITH 1994–2005	CATHY VESPER-WILSON 1995–2001
LESLIE KING 1961–1962	SIDNEY FOX 1965–1968	ELLEN STINCHFIELD 1972–1980	CHARLES BRUMMEL 1979–1985	KEELI (KIRKPATRICK) CROOK 1986–1988	KATHY GROSSMAN 1994–2000	CLARA RADCLIFFE 2003–2007
G.E. ALBERTSON 1961–1967	WILLIAM E. WALSH 1966–1970	LEONARD FARR 1972–1980	SHELDON MEYER 1980–1989	RON HJORT 1987–1994	DOROTHY HEAGY 1992–2001	HARRY ABEL 2003–
HENRY F. HANSEN 1961–1965	RALPH STULLER 1966–1973	STEPHEN MILLER 1974–1974	JON DOWERS 1980–1984	HUGH HARRISON 1988–1989	KAY HEIKKILA 1992–1998	CHERIE MITCHELL 2005–
WILFRED A. JORDAN 1961–1963	THOMAS GUERIN 1967–1969	DOLORES FURMAN 1974–1977	DOUGLAS N. MILLS 1981–1982	TONI POOLE 1988–1994	DAVID BRIDGHAM 1998–	LONNY ANDERSON 2005–
KARL GEHLERT 1962–1979	MAXINE MAUNEY 1967–1972	BARBARA LEA BROWN 1974–1985	MARCELLA DAILEY 1981–1989	RON KRESKEY 1989–1997	MARCIA JENSEN 2000–	RICK HOWELL 2007–
BEN R. CHANDLER 1962–1972	SAM DEMENT 1967–1969	RICHARD MAEYAERT 1974–1978	JON LITTLEFIELD 1982–1994	CLINT LAIRD 1989–1999	MIKE MURRAY 2001–2005	
RICHARD HANEN 1962–1964	ROBERT DETLEFSEN 1969–1978	LOUIS LORENZ 1977–1981	MARK HAMLIN 1984–1992	KATY EYMANN 1989–1992	CAROL OELKE 2001–2009	
HARRY BYRER 1963–1967	LLOYD KUNI 1970–1978	GORDON ROSS 1978–1986	DONNA BROWN 1985–1987	CHARLIE VINCENT 1999–2003	NANCY BROUHARD 1994–2003	

Southwestern Oregon Community College Board of Education Members from 1961 to present.

APPENDIX

Throughout the interviews that supported some of the content of this 50-year celebration, there were consistent themes that rose to the surface when individuals were asked about the one thing that impressed them most about their time at SWOCC; here are a few of their answers:

Phill Anderson – Dean of Instruction 1966-1999 – *"SWOCC fulfilled and modified my dream. When I was a kid around 10 years of age, I used to listen to the radio program called the Halls of Ivy. Ronald Coleman was a college professor in an Ivy League School and for some reason that caught my imagination and made me want to be a college professor; I didn't want to be a cowboy or a fireman, I wanted to be a college professor. My dream was modified because I did everything at SWOCC, so I saw it from every perspective. I saw the culture of the campus as caring for students as educated people; being concerned about their needs, not necessarily about their wants."*

Dr. Bob Barber – President 1985-1990 – *"Prior to coming to SWOCC, I worked in the Connecticut college system where the 12 community colleges were controlled and run by the State Office of Community Colleges. I knew that the Oregon Community colleges were true community colleges where decisions were made locally and the community provided the majority of the support – until the passage of Ballot Measure 5."*

Bob Bower – Professor of English 1971-2008 – *"Helping of those people who for whatever reasons were financially or educationally impaired to be successful either in vocational or transfer programs. You can look into their eyes and know they were grateful."*

Don Burdg – Math Professor 1967-1994 – *"One thing Margaret and I fondly remember about the early years of SWOCC was that every Friday after payday the faculty and staff would meet in a Happy Hour at some faculty/staff home for snacks and conversation. That was great in that we got to not only see where others lived but got to converse with those whom we did not see often on campus. The faculty/staff eventually grew too large for this sort of thing and it was eventually dropped. I have been on the campuses of all the community colleges in Oregon and believe that, without a doubt, the SWOCC campus is the most beautiful of the bunch."*

Barbara Davey – Director of Nursing 1976–2007 – *"The nursing program at SWOCC was rigorous and our graduates are highly respected in the industry. I am very proud of the growth in the number of male nurses that graduated from our program."*

Barbara Dodrill – Business Professor 1994-2001 – (Barbara is probably the only teacher in all of Oregon who graduated from the telegrapher's school in Montana – as she explained it, this was during World War II and when the phone lines went down they reverted to using the telegraph for taking orders for the train. She also was in charge of handing the mail bag to the trip trains for the Milwaukee Railroad - as the "train came rumbling through." The train never slowed down and she never missed a pick nor was ever knocked off her feet as she hung on to a nearby pole for dear life!) – *"I felt quite privileged to teach at*

SWOCC. When I joined the faculty in the early 1970s it was small and very close knit. We were all really focused on doing what was best for the students. The retreat at camp Myrtlewood solidified the relationships between all levels of the campus community and allowed me to know who all the players were that made the campus run smoothly. My hope was that my work at SWOCC might just provide a new level of hope for a student."

Mike Gaudette – Dean of College Advancement/Foundation Director 1991-2006 – *"When my wife and I came for an interview on campus, my conclusion was that I would love to work here. I loved the natural beauty of the area, great people and a community that was similar to the area from which we had been living in Washington. My proudest moments were around the things we (Dr. Kridelbaugh and me) were able to do and the strategies we came up with to expand the physical campus in new and creative ways. We used no capital construction money from the State to expand the footprint. When I was hired, my title was Director of College Advancement which included managing and growing the SWOCC Foundation and writing grants for the College – and that fit my interest and background. Over time my duties grew both horizontally and vertically and I retired as the Director of the SWOCC Foundation and Dean of College Advancement."*

Holly Hall – Student 1971 – *"The administration was accessible, the professors were accessible, you didn't have to feel like you needed special permission to just be yourself and pursue your education as you wanted. You did not have to fit into the slot like you might at the university. You could have the slot fit around you."*

Mark Hamlin – Associated Student Body President and Board Member 1984-1992 – *"There was an acknowledgement that not every student graduating from a vocational program would remain in the area, but there was satisfaction knowing that the College had met a need and that the son or daughter or unemployed could afford to better themselves close to home. The community recognized the importance of this resource in their backyard. The College worked."*

Fred Harris – Student 1961-1962 – *"What I like about SWOCC is it afforded me a career change and completely changed my life and that of my family for the better. Forty-eight years later I can't think of anything I would have changed; it was what it was and it worked."*

Kirk Jones – College Librarian 1970-1998 – *"What is really good about SWOCC is the bang for the buck. It is good value. It is the cheapest way to get going – less tuition and that is particularly important in today's economy. Every time a mill would close, you could see the enrollment at the College increase."*

Dr. Steve Kridelbaugh – President 1990-2005 – *"During my tenure at the College, I spent an inordinate share of my time insuring that there would be adequate funding to expand the College and provide the very best two-year education for students I could."*

Bill Lemoine – Professor of Forestry 1968-1997 – *"One of my fondest memories of my 29 years at SWOCC involved going out to visit my students on their work site and see them as successful contributors to the profession. Another was the fact* *that the administration at the College gave us a pretty free hand to run our programs, I liked that independence."*

Jon Littlefield – Board Member and Chair 1982-1992 – *"One of the joys I remember was the opportunity to hand out the diplomas at graduation. As I watched a 40-something retrained displaced worker walk across the stage to receive his diploma, I might see out of the corner of my eye his aging mother with tears of pride streaming down her face, a spouse whose family security would be improved and teenage children not particularly paying attention until their father walked on stage. Sometime I could hardly get out the word 'Congratulations.'"*

Dr. Sheldon Meyer – Vice President of Administrative Services 1993-2008 – Dr. Meyer's story is worthy of capturing it in its entirety as it reflects the impact that an institution like SWOCC can have on an individual's life – *"I grew up in Coos Bay, graduated from Marshfield in 1961. I enrolled at the University of Oregon and flunked out in two terms, mainly due to the fact that I started a Rock and Roll band that played in the surrounding towns every weekend. I then transferred down to Southwestern Oregon College in the spring of '62, because the U of O told me that I wasn't ready to be there anymore. And during that first term at SWOCC, I earned a 0.25 GPA; carrying 12 credit hours. My downfall that Spring quarter was due to the fact that I was going to take three final exams on the same Friday that the local high school was having its graduation party and I said 'to hell with the exams, let's go'; so I never took the finals. Lillian Van Loan, the wife of the college president at the time, was teaching Psychology and she flunked me! My parents said I probably was not cut out for college and would therefore no longer fund my education."* (Sheldon seemed to be the only person who had contact with every president at SWOCC.)

Sheldon returned to SWOCC in the fall of 1965, became the student body vice president, carried a heavy academic load with a GPA of nearly 4.0 and graduated in 1967. *"I remember the student lounge was a temporary facility in what looked like a mobile home located just east of Sitkum Hall. After I graduated from SWOCC I followed my advisor to the University of Utah and received a BS degree before returning to Coos Bay to take a job as a truant officer for all of Coos County for a couple of years. John Rulifson, dean of instruction, encouraged me to continue my education so I enrolled at OSU in a counseling program where I received my master's and PhD. I taught courses at the University of Oregon before returning to Coos Bay and eventually ended up in hospital administration at the Bay Area Hospital and at that time ran for a seat on the SWOCC Board of Education. I started working at SWOCC in 1993 where I stayed for the next 17 years retiring in 2008. I was on the College Board of Education from 1980-1989."*

Bob Miller – Professor of Accounting 1972-1997 – *"When I came to SWOCC, we didn't have all the buildings that are there now and we were a tight knit group like a family. Once a month we would have a Friday night get together. There were all kinds of communication between disciplines. I knew all the administrators by their first names. It was really a community and I liked that term, because it signified the way the campus ran."*

Don Moffitt – Professor of Business 1961-1980 – *"I see the College being the major trainer of people for the work world; I think that's the main thrust (of SWOCC) as opposed to a lower division transfer route for the students."* (64)

Eric Muller – Professor of English 1969-1986 – *"Best for me were the eager students, good course variety, and thoughtful colleagues and the College added a heady mix to a fairly homogenous population, and that mix energized theater, music, and graphic arts especially. And it opens doors for the traditionally underprepared."*

Deb Nicholls – Executive Assistant 1987 to Present – *"Southwestern has been a great place to go to school and especially to work. The South Coast is incredibly beautiful and a wonderful area to raise a family. Graduation is the highlight of the year for me. It's so exciting to see the all the pomp and circumstance and the culmination of the students' hard work as they walk across the stage!"*

John Noland – Creative Writing Professor 1971-2001 – *"During one of the College's accreditation reviews, the visiting accreditation committee knew all about The Beacon's record and wanted to see how we functioned. They seemed to think we must have a big room with lots of expensive equipment or something. Of course, we didn't. We had only determination, well-trained editors and hard-working students."*

Karen Pringle – Foundation Executive Director 2010 to Present – *"In Coos and Curry counties, people can give a gift of education that keeps on giving for a lifetime."*

Dr. Clara Radcliffe – Professor of English 1981-2001 – *"Eleven years ago, I began teaching at SWOCC, but thought what I really wanted to do was teach in a four-year college or university. While on the University campus doing post doctoral work, I felt something was missing – it was my love for the SWOCC campus and teaching. It was the lovely campus set in some of the world's most beautiful country and in love with those colleagues who cared so much about teaching, in love with the students who are often so eager and sometimes too scared, students who come in such a wonderful variety of ages, interests, backgrounds and ambitions"* (72)

Dr. Patty Scott – President 2008 to Present – *"The community college deals with all types of students. We have an open door policy to all students from every walk of life – from 18 year olds to 88 year olds. Giving people second chances - that is what we are all about. The reason I have stayed at SWOCC all these years is that I have never gotten bored. I was hired by SWOCC back in 1993 to work on retention by developing programs for students. I am still passionate about keeping the campus vibrant so students want to come here and complete this part of their post-secondary education."*

Peter Sorensen – Student 1970-1971 – *"One of my favorite memories, as a junior high or high school kid, was the summer gatherings of people connected to the College. They used to have these on the North Spit and we'd take small boats from Charleston over to the North Spit. We'd spend the whole day, getting crabs and clams and having a big BBQ. The early leaders of the College would have Board members, the College president, senior staff, all of the staff, faculty and invited student leaders – and all of the kids of those people. It was great!*

"The community college system is a phenomenal idea that bridges the gap in American education. Somehow we inherited the positive part of the British educational system whereby we should have post-secondary education for the leaders of society and they should go to college and they should learn great literature and be big thinkers, but they forgot the other half of our educational system where you need to have phenomenal crafts people that know how to read, etc. and to make a society work you need to have everybody. This was left out of America's first 100 years of educational development."

John Speasl – Athletic Director 1973-2011 – *"This is really a great place to work and that I was having an influence on people's lives. After being on campus for ten years, I realized that I never thanked my coach for influencing me in a direction that I have happily pursued now at SWOCC for 38 years. So I wrote him a two page letter thanking him."* (On November 6, 2010, the College named the basketball/volleyball floor of Prosper Hall – "Speasl Court" in recognition of his long leadership of the athletic programs at SWOCC). *"Many of my student-athletes came back for the celebration and some came up to thank me for what I had done for them. So, I guess my parting comment would be that I hope that in some small way that some of my philosophy of life has rubbed off on my students to make them better people."*

Veneita Stender – Associate Professor of Home Economics 1965-1991 – *"I primarily taught women as my classes focused on clothing and home economic skills. It was my belief and that of Jack Brookins that – if you educated a woman, you educated an entire family. I truly loved my work whatever it was. The campus had a family feeling, especially when the faculty was so small with lots of social activities among the whole group. It was a tremendous opportunity for me to pursue what I wanted to do."*

Susan Walker – Director of Nursing 1990 to Present – *"I too am proud of our program particularly at the very high pass rate our students acquire when taking the RN exam. When we adopted the Oregon Consortium for Nursing Education (OCNE) a stronger bond was developed with the four-year universities, especially OHSU."*

Dr. Wendell Van Loan – President 1961-1965 – *"Wherever I go, I am asked two questions – When are you going to have a football team, and when are you going to become a four-year college? To the first question, I answer, we don't want a football team; we'll leave that to the high schools in the district. And we'll leave the four-year programs to the already established four-year institutions in Oregon. What we are interested in is a two-year vocational-technical program and quality education for students who are interested in academic work. Each man and woman should have the opportunity to do the thing they do best. You shouldn't try to force everyone to be a college professor anymore than you should force everyone to be a plumber."* [54]

Presidents of Southwestern Oregon Community College

Dr. Wendell Van Loan – 1961-1965

Dr. Wendell L. Van Loan came to SWOCC as its first president in 1961 and is credited with helping the College Board of Education select the current campus site at Empire Lakes. Before coming to SWOCC he was a professor of Education at Oregon State University in Corvallis. He received his bachelor's and master's degrees from Oregon State University and his doctorate in Education from Stanford University. His wife, Lillian, who was a professor of Psychology at OSU, joined her husband as a professor of Psychology at SWOCC. In May 1965, both left SWOCC to accept professorships at the University of Oregon.

Jack E. Brookins – 1965-1985

Jack Brookins came to SWOCC in 1964 to head the Technical/Vocational division of the College. Before coming to SWOCC, he served as coordinator for class instructors at Oakland City College in Oakland, California. He received his bachelor's degree in Trade and Industrial Education from Colorado State University (CSU) in 1950; his master's in Administration and Supervision of Vocational Education from CSU and at the time he came to SWOCC was working on his doctorate from the University of California at Berkley but never finished it.

Dr. Robert Barber – 1985-1990

Dr. Robert Barber came to SWOCC in 1985 as its third president. Before that he was dean of instruction at Mohegan Community College in Norwich, Connecticut, and held a variety of other positions in community colleges in Connecticut. He was an inner-city special education teacher, working with emotionally disturbed youth. From 1966 to 1971, he served as the department head of Destroyer Engineering for the U.S. Navy. Dr. Barber earned his bachelor's degree from Cornell University in Economics in 1966; his master's in Education from State University of New York at Albany; and a doctorate in Education Administration from the University of Connecticut.

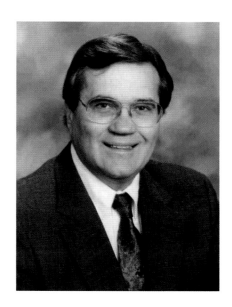

Dr. Stephen Kridelbaugh – 1990-2005

Dr. Stephen Kridelbaugh served as the fourth president of Southwestern Oregon Community College from September 1990 to July 2005. Prior to coming to Southwestern Dr. Kridelbaugh served as president of Olney Central College in Olney, Illinois, from 1985 to 1990 and in a multitude of instructional and administrative capacities at Lower Columbia College in Longview, Washington, from 1974 to 1985. He received his bachelor's degree in Geology from Wayne State University in Detroit, Michigan, and his Ph.D. in Geology from the University of Colorado in 1971. Dr. Kridelbaugh served as assistant professor of Geology at Eastern Washington State University in 1971 and pursued primary geochemical research of lunar rocks and soils at the Center for Volcanology at the University of Oregon from 1972 to 1974. Dr. Kridelbaugh also served in Africa with the United States Department of State in Bamako, Republic of Mali, and the United States Army.

Dr. Judith Hansen – 2005-2008

Dr. Judith Hansen joined SWOCC in 2005 as its fourth president. She served in that position until 2008. Before coming to SWOCC, she was the president of Independence Community College in Kansas. Her previous community college experience included serving as executive vice president of Waubonsee Community College in Chicago, Illinois and president of Olney Central College in Olney, Illinois. Dr. Hansen is a graduate of Iowa State University where she received her bachelor's degree in Sociology, master's degree in Counseling and Ph.D. in Higher Education.

Dr. Patty Scott – 2008-Present

Dr. Patty M. Scott has been at Southwestern Oregon Community College since 1993. She started out at Southwestern splitting time as director of Student Support Services (TRIO) and Counseling Faculty. She was named director of Educational Support Programs in 2002 and served as dean of students from February of 2006 until being named as interim president in October 2008. During her tenure at Southwestern, Patty served a five-year stint on the Faculty Senate and spent three of those as chair. She received an Excellence in Action award in 2005 for her work as chair of a faculty led retention taskforce that resulted in creation of several new programs and campus cultural change. Dr. Scott became the sixth president of SWOCC on December 14, 2009.

After starting her higher education pursuit at Lane Community College in Eugene, Patty completed a bachelor's degree in Sociology from the University of Oregon. She went on to earn a Master of Arts degree in College Student Personnel Administration from Bowling Green State University in Ohio and Doctorate of Education in Community College Leadership from Oregon State University.

Patty is very involved in the community. She served on the steering committee for Leadership Coos for 14 years, is a trainer for the Ford Family Leadership program, a Parks Commissioner with City of Coos Bay, on the Foundation Board of Bay Area Hospital, budget committee for Coos Bay-North Bend Water Board, and is a member of Rotary and Zonta service clubs.

Prior to coming to Southwestern, Patty worked in student services at the University of Oregon and in Career Services at Roger Williams College (now University) in Bristol, Rhode Island.

SOUTHWESTERN OREGON COMMUNITY COLLEGE – CAPITAL CONSTRUCTION

Building	Year Built	Square Feet	Original Cost	Original Use
PHASE 1				
Randolph Hall	1964	12,836	$183,263	Computer Services, Classrooms, Offices
Umpqua Hall	1964	11,680	$264,593	Automotive Technology
PHASE 2				
Coaledo Hall	1965	9,800	$263,206	Science Labs, Classrooms, Offices
Dellwood Hall	1965	9,375	$221,209	Student Services, Offices
Maintenance	1965	4,712	$20,000	Workshops, Storage, Offices
Sitkum Hall	1965	10,240	$208,897	Classrooms, Offices
PHASE 3				
Prosper Hall	1967	25,835	$538,679	Gym, Offices
Tioga Hall	1969	56,144	$1,631,520	Offices, Computer Lab, Library, Print Shop
PHASE 4				
B-2	1974	1,800	$35,000	Wrestling
B-3	1974	3,200	$45,174	Storage
Fire Training	1974	1,800	$24,273	Fire Program, Offices, Storage, Truck Garage
(Apprenticeship)	1978	720	$40,158	Offices
Empire Hall	1980	17,189	$1,354,545	Cafeteria, Meeting Rooms, Offices
Fire Tower	1981	852	$17,220	Fire Training
Eden Hall	1982	8,440	$663,890	Art Workshops, Classrooms, Offices, Auditorium
Fairview Hall	1982	15,400	$942,587	Machine/Welding Shops, Offices
Lampa Hall	1982	3,760	$290,244	Offices
Sumner Hall	1982	8,440	$663,890	Nursing/Forestry Programs, Classrooms, Offices
Sunset Hall	1982	6,840	$302,400	Music Program, Offices, Performance Hall
Stensland Hall	1995	14,041	$1,163,973	Bookstore, Offices, Classrooms
Newmark Center	1996	35,242	$3,710,000	Offices, Classrooms, State Services
Athletic Field House	1997	4,800	$67,725	Baseball/Softball Practice
Family Center	1997	5,798	$624,598	Child Care Center, Offices
Housing Depot	1997	3,963	$400,000	
Housing Units (Phase I)	1997	39,555	$3,200,000	8 Resident Student Apartment Buildings
Housing Units (Phase II)	1998	10,558	$840,000	2 Resident Student Apartment Buildings
Housing Units (Phase III)	2000	21,318	$2,200,000	4 Resident Student Apartment Buildings
Performing Arts Center	2001	21,890	$3,800,000	Theater
OCCI	2004	15,000	$2,734,571	Culinary Classes
Housing Units (Phase IV)	2005	31,954	$5,200,000	4 – Three-Story Student Apartment Buildings
Recreation Center	2005	41,000	$4,962,400	Gym, Classroooms
Brookings Curry Campus	1960s	5,700	$164,000	Classrooms, Offices, Computer Lab
New Curry County Campus	2011	26,800	$8,300,000	Classrooms, Offices, Labs, Meeting Rooms, Bookstore, Student Services
Totals		**480,982**	**$44,914,015**	

The Original College Faculty in 1961

Full-time and part-time:

Anthony Arrambide – Modern Languages

Wayne Andrews – Automotive Technology

James A. Becker – Electrical Apprentice training

Maurine Bayes – Business Education

Robert C. Croft – Librarian, Social Sciences

Clara M. Eickworth – Home Economics

Helen W. Ferguson – Business Education

William J. Holmes – Physical Education

Tom Humphrey – English and Literature

Charles W. Korburger, Jr. - Director of Collegiate Division

Ellsworth J. Leegard– Welding

Ronald Lilienthal – Science

Donald R. Moffitt – Chairman of Business Education Department

William L. Orr – Business Administration

Robert A. Osborne – Mathematics

Maurice M. Romig – Director of Technical-Vocational Education

Lyle Shibley – Driver Training

Roger Spaugh – Electronics Technology

Veneita Stender – Home Economics

David L. Trembley – Electronics

Margaret E. Trussell – Social Science

Lillian Schroeder Van Loan – Psychology

Elisabeth Van Ryckevorsel – Languages

Larry J. Whitney – Chairman Technical Division

Theodore R. Willard – Business Education

2009-2010 Budget – All Funds

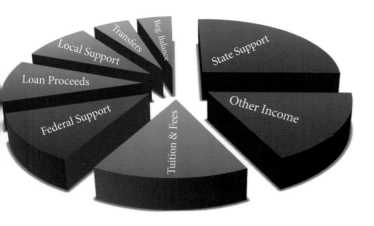

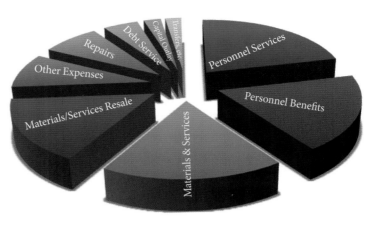

RESOURCES

■ State Support	26%
■ Other Income	17%
■ Tuition and Fees	15%
■ Federal Support	12%
■ Loan Proceeds	10%
■ Local Support	9%
■ Transfers from Other Funds	6%
■ Est. Beginning Fund Balance	5%

REQUIREMENTS

■ Personnel Services	22%
■ Personnel Benefits	19%
■ Materials and Services	18%
■ Materials/Services Resale	16%
■ Other Expenses	9%
■ Repairs	8%
■ Debt Service	4%
■ Capital Outlay	2%
■ Transfers/Contingency/ Unappropriated Fund	2%

SWOCC Enrollment History by group

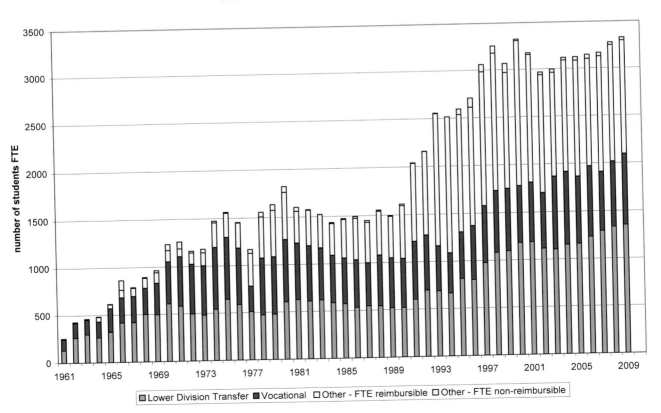

MANUFACTURING VS. NON-MANUFACTURING JOBS IN COOS AND CURRY COUNTIES

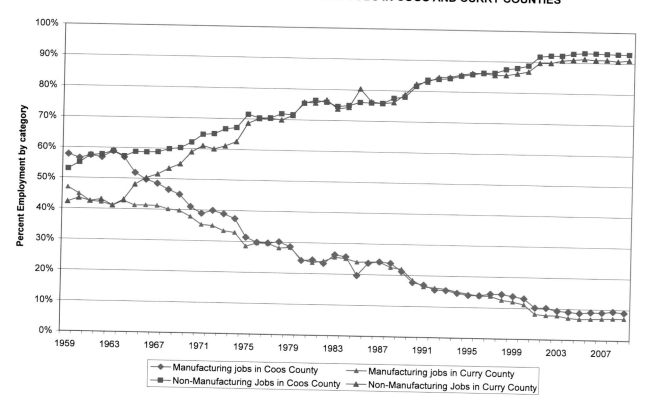

Legend:
- Manufacturing jobs in Coos County
- Manufacturing jobs in Curry County
- Non-Manufacturing Jobs in Coos County
- Non-Manufacturing Jobs in Curry County

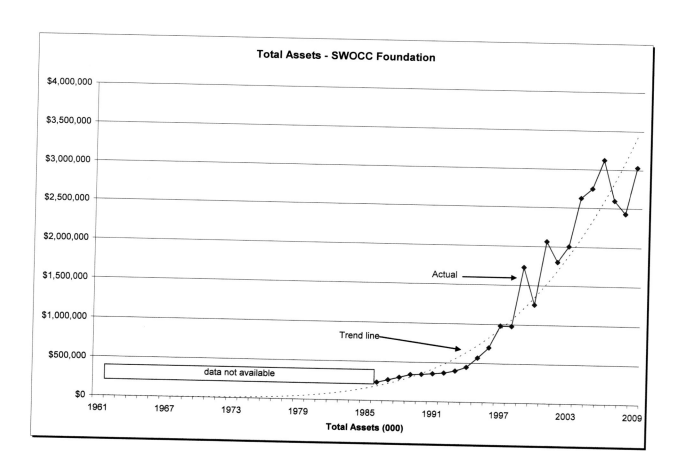

Total Assets - SWOCC Foundation

Sports History at SWOCC

1960s Championships
1964 Men's Track Champions OCCAA – Bill Horning Coach
1965 Wrestling Co-OCCAA Champions – Bill Horning Coach
1966 Men's Cross Country OCCAA Champions – Bill Horning Coach
1967 Men's Cross Country OCCAA Champions – Bill Horning Coach
1968 Men's Golf OCCAA Champions – Jim Ferguson Coach
1969 Men's Golf OCCAA Champions – Jim Ferguson Coach

Coaches in the '60s
Dale Bates – Men's Basketball 1967-68 to 1972-73 and Athletic Director 1967-68 to 1972-73
Berge Borevick – Men's Basketball 1964-65 to 1966-67 and Athletic Director 1964-65 to 1966-67
Jim Ferguson – Men's Golf 1967-68 to 1968-69
Bill Holmes – First Men's Basketball Coach, Men's Basketball and Athletic Director 1961-62 to 1963-64
Bill Horning – Track and Field and Wrestling 1964-65 to 1969-70, Cross Country and Baseball 1966-67 to1969-70

Sports in the '60s
Baseball 1966 to Present (dropped in 1975 to 1994)
Men's Basketball 1961-62 to Present
Cross Country 1964 to Present (dropped from 1981 to 2005)
Men's Golf 1967-68 to Present (dropped from 1969 to 1998 and again from 1999 to 2003)
Track and Field 1964 to Present
Wrestling 1964 to Present (dropped from 1987to 1995)

Teams started competing in Prosper Hall in 1967-68

1970s Championships
1974 Men's Basketball OCCAA Champions – Chuck Francis Coach
1979 Men's Basketball OCCAA Champions – Terry Stahel Coach
1978 Women's Tennis OCCAA Champions – Terry Stahel Coach

Coaches in the '70s
Dale Bates (See Coaches in the '60s)
Bob Bower – Wrestling 1970-71
Don Burdg – Tennis 1972-73 to 1978-79
Chuck Francis – Men's Basketball 1973-74 to 1976-77 and 1973-74 to 1976-77
Dave Hengstellar – Wrestling 1978-79
Mike Hodges – Cross Country 1970-71 to 1990-81, Track and Field 1970-71 to 1985-86
        and Athletic Director 1981-82 to 1985-96
Bill Horning (See Coaches in the '60s)
Darwin Lovell – Men's Tennis 1979-80
Tony Macias – Wrestling 1971-72 to 1972-73
Harold Martin – Baseball 1970-71 to 1974-75
Charlie McClure – Women's Basketball 1979-80
Cheri Robinson – First Women's Athletic Coach, Women's Basketball and Volleyball 1977-78 to1978-79
John Speasl – Wrestling 1973-74 to 1976-77, 1978-79 to 1986-87, 1996-96 to 1996-97, Volleyball 1979-80 to 2011
        and Athletic Director 1986-87 to 2011
Terry Stahel – Men's Basketball 1977-78 to 1980-81, Women's Tennis 1979-80
        and Athletic Director 1977-78 to 1980-81

Women's Athletics were started in 1978-79 school year (volleyball and basketball)

Sports in the '70s

Baseball (See Sports in the '60s)
Men's Basketball (See Sports in the '60s)
Women's Basketball 1978 to Present
Cross Country (See Sports in the '60s)
Tennis 1972-73 to 1980-81
Track and Field (See Sports in the '60s)
Volleyball 1978 to Present
Wrestling (See Sports in the '60s)

1980s Championships

1980 Wrestling OCCAA Champions – John Speasl Coach
1981 Wrestling OCCAA Champions – John Speasl Coach
1985 Volleyball NWAACC Southern Region Champion – John Speasl Coach
1989 Volleyball NWAACC Conference 4th place – John Speasl Coach

Coaches in the '80s

Mary Bailey – Tennis 1980-81
Bruce Case – Men's Basketball 1981-82 to 1983-84
Dan Cumberland – Women's Basketball 1980-81 to 1985-86
Hunter Fales – Women's Basketball 1988-89 to 2003-04 and Men's & Women's Track and Field – 1986-87 to 1990-91
Mike Hodges (See Coaches from the '70s)
Jim Krause – Men's Basketball 1984-85
Jeff Menday – Men's Basketball 1985-86 to 1988-89
Tom Nicholls – Men's Basketball 1989-90 to 1996-97, 1999-00 to 2002-03
        Women's Basketball – 2004-05 to 2005-06
John Speasl (See Coaches from the '70s)
Terry Stahel (See Coaches from the '70s)
Ken Tedder – Women's Basketball 1986-87 to 1987-88

Sports in the '80s

Men's & Women's Basketball (See Sports in the '60s and '70s)
Men's & Women's Cross Country (See Sports in the '60s)
Men's & Women's Tennis (See Sports in the '70s)
Track and Field (See Sports in the '60s)
Volleyball (See Sports in the '70s)
Wrestling (See Sports in the '60s)

1990s Championships

1990 Volleyball NWAACC Conference 2nd place – John Speasl Coach
1992 Volleyball NWAACC Conference 4th place – John Speasl Coach
1997 Softball NWAACC Conference 4th place – Charlie Christiansen Coach
1999 Women's Golf NWAACC Southern Region Champions – Iain Karroll Coach

Coaches in the' 90s

Jeff Ahmann – Men's Basketball 1997-98 to 1998-99
Charlie Christiansen – Softball 1994-95 to 1996-97
Mike Duffy – Softball 1997-98, 2006-07, and Women's Basketball 2006-07
Hunter Fales (See Coaches from the '80s)
Jennifer Franklin – Softball 1998-99 to 2005-06
Bill Hatch – Baseball 1994-95 to 1997-98
Tony Jones – Wrestling 1997-98 to 2000-01

Iain Karroll – Men's & Women's Golf 1998-99
Shaun Kohn – Men's & Women's Soccer 1997-98 and Women's Soccer 2003-04 to 2007-08
Dan Neal – Men's & Women's Track and Field 1991-92 to Present and Cross Country 2005-06 to Present
Tom Nicholls (See Coaches from the '80s)
Joel Perkins – Women's Soccer 1998-99 to 2001-02 and Men's Basketball 2003-04 to 2004-05
Jeremiah Robbins – Baseball 1998-99 to 2000-01
John Speasl (See Coaches from the '70s)
Cengiz Yakut – Men's Soccer 1998-99 to 2000-01

Sports in the '90s
Baseball (See Sports in the '60s)
Men's & Women's Basketball (See Sports in the '60s)
Men's Golf (See Sports in the '60s)
Women's Golf 1998-99 to Present (dropped in 1999 to 2003)
Men's & Women's Soccer 1997 to Present
Softball 1994-95 to Present
Track and Field (See Sports in the '60s)
Volleyball (See Sports in the '70s)
Wrestling (See Sports in the '60s)

2000s Championships
2000 Men's Basketball NWAACC Southern Region Champions – Tom Nicholls Coach
2000 Men's Basketball NWAACC Conference 3rd Place – Tom Nicholls Coach
2002 Men's Basketball NWAACC Southern Region Champions – Tom Nicholls Coach
2005 Men's Golf NWAACC Conference 3rd Place – Marie Simonds Coach
2005 Volleyball NWAACC Southern Region Co-Champions – John Speasl Coach
2006 Men's Golf NWAACC Conference 3rd Place – Marie Simonds Coach
2006 Women's Golf NWAACC Conference 3rd Place – Marie Simonds Coach
2006 Women's Soccer NWAACC Southern Region Champions – Shaun Kohn Coach
2006 Women's Soccer NWAACC Conference 3rd Place – Shaun Kohn Coach
2007 Wrestling NJCAA National Championships 7th Place – Adam Whitlatch Coach
2007 Combined Cross Country NWAACC Conference 4th Place – Dan Neal Coach
2007 Women's Cross Country NWAACC Conference 4th Place – Dan Neal Coach
2009 Men's Golf NWAACC Conference Champions – Michael Chupka Coach
2009 Softball NWAACC Conference 3rd Place – Megan Corriea Coach
2010 Softball NWAACC Conference 2nd Place – Megan Corriea Coach

Coaches in the 2000s
Cole Brandeburg – Women's Soccer 2008-09 to 2010
Michael Chupka – Men's & Women's Golf 2008-09
Megan Corriea – Softball 2007-08 to Present
Mike Duffy (See Coaches from the '90s)
Daniel Esposito – Baseball 2007-11
Ray Fabien – Men's Soccer – 2006-07 to Present and Golf 2009-10 to Present
Corky Franklin – Baseball 2001-02 to 2006-07
Jen Franklin (See Coaches from the '90s)
Mike Herbert – Women's Basketball 2008-09 to Present
Trevor Hoppe – Men's Basketball 2005-06 to Present
Tony Jones (See Coaches from the '90s)
Shaun Kohn (See Coaches from the '90s)

Oregon's Community Colleges [3]

District:	Formation Date:
Southwestern Oregon	May 1, 1961
Treasure Valley	November 2, 1961
Central Oregon	January 30, 1962
Blue Mountain	June 8, 1962
Umpqua	March 30, 1964
Lane	October 19, 1964
Mt. Hood	June 12, 1965
Clackamas	May 24, 1966
Linn-Benton	December 6, 1966
Clatsop	January 26, 1967
Portland	June 5, 1968
Chemeketa	September 23, 1969
Rogue	November 3, 1970
Treaty Oak (Columbia Gorge)	November 2, 1976
Tillamook Bay	March 31, 1981
Oregon Coast	May 19, 1987
Klamath	May 21, 1996

ASG Presidents

1961-1962	William Gordon		1986-1987	Ken Ocobock
1962-1963	Benny Young		1987-1988	Dean Huard
1963-1964	Royce Wright		1988-1989	Brent Harvey (Resigned) Joe Patnode
1964-1965	Jerry Coffindaffer		1989-1990	Patty Hoppins
1965-1966	David Rudin		1990-1991	Marie Head (Resigned) Terry Sherman
1966-1967	Rodney Hickenlooper		1991-1992	Terry Sherman
1967-1968	Dennis Ahlstrom		1992-1993	Nick Long
1968-1969	Bill Clawson		1993-1994	Celeste Hobson
1969-1970	Dan Gammon		1994-1995	Dawn Albro
1970-1971	Peggy Paul		1995-1996	Andrew Prather
1971-1972	Dave Hudson		1996-1997	Jason Culver
1972-1973	Giles Larrabee		1997-1998	Casey Budesilich
1973-1974	Sara Meade		1998-1999	Robert Manske
1974-1975	Ken Kay		1999-2000	David DeVriend
1975-1976	Mark Paxson		2000-2001	Ryan Elza
1976-1977	Stephen Riley		2001-2002	Iosha Hodgson-Reed
1977-1978	Gerald Burgess		2002-2003	Chad Smith
1978-1979	Kevin McCarthy		2003-2004	Tracey Curlee
1979-1980	Bob Jones		2004-2005	Amy Hills
1980-1981	Mark Hamlin		2005-2006	Travis Osborn
1981-1982	David Hinkle		2006-2007	Holly Egan
1982-1983	Becky Garino		2007-2008	Megan Franko
1983-1984	Kay Schirmer		2008-2009	Drew Jones
1984-1985	Diana Larsen		2009-2010	Cody Carlson
1985-1986	Nadine Shumake		2010-2011	Caitlin Portinga

Degrees Earned by Graduates (2010-2011)

Degree Name		Count	Total 370
AAS	ADMINISTRATIVE OFFICE PROFESSIONAL	1	
AAS	COMPUTER INFORMATION SYSTEMS	1	
AAS	CULINARY ARTS	34	
AAS	EMT PARAMEDIC TECHNOLOGY	8	
AAS	WELDING AND FABRICATION	8	
AAS	HUMAN SERVICES	2	
AAS	ACCOUNTING	3	
AAS	BAKING AND PASTRY	23	
AAS	CHILDHOOD EDUCATION AND FAMILY STUDIES	6	
AAS	CRIMINAL JUSTICE LAW ENFORCEMENT ADMINISTRATION	3	
AAS	FIRE SCIENCE TECHNOLOGY	8	
AAS	GERONTOLOGY	1	
AAS	INDUSTRIAL TECHNOLOGY (APPRENTICESHIP)	1	
AAS	OFFICE MANAGEMENT	1	
AAS	SMALL BUSINESS ENTREPRENEURSHIP	5	
AAS	COMPUTER INFORMATION SYSTEMS: SOFTWARE SUPPORT	1	
AAS	MEDICAL ASSISTANT	7	
AAS	NETWORK DESIGN AND ADMINISTRATION	5	
AAS	NURSING	21	
AGS	GENERAL STUDIES	20	
AS	CRIMINAL JUSTICE EMPHASIS	2	
AS	ENGINEERING EMPHASIS	1	
AS	NATURAL SCIENCE EMPHASIS	1	
ASOT	BUSINESS	12	
ASSOCIATE OF ARTS/OREGON TRANSFER		124	
ASSOCIATE OF SCIENCE DEGREE		18	
BASIC TECHNICAL SKILLS IN HUMAN SERVICES		4	
BOOKKEEPING CLERICAL CERTIFICATE		1	
CERTIFICATE OF COMPLETION GROUP EXERCISE LEADER		3	
CERTIFICATE OF COMPLETION COMPUTER INFORMATION SYSTEMS		1	
CERTIFICATE OF COMPLETION FIRE SCIENCE TECH: LEVEL 2		1	
CERTIFICATE OF COMPLETION PERSONAL TRAINER/AGING ADULT		1	
CERTIFICATE OF COMPLETION PHARMACY TECHNICIAN		5	
CERTIFICATE OF COMPLETION PHLEBOTOMY TECHNICIAN		1	
CERTIFICATE OF COMPLETION WELDING AND FABRICATION		4	
COMPUTER TECHNICIAN CERTIFICATE		1	
COMPUTER TECHNICIAN EXAM PREP CERTIFICATE		3	
CORE CONCEPTS IN HUMAN SERVICES		2	
JUVENILE CORRECTIONS CERTIFICATE		1	
MEDICAL AIDE		1	
MEDICAL CLERICAL CERTIFICATE		4	
NETWORK CERTIFICATION EXAM PREP CERTIFICATE		3	
NETWORK FUNDAMENTALS CERTIFICATE		2	
NETWORK TECHNICIAN CERTIFICATE		2	
OREGON TRANSFER MODULE		1	
PATHWAYS CERT. COMP.: CCENT CERTIFICATION PREPARATION		2	
PATHWAYS CERT. COMP.: CCNA CERTIFICATION PREPARATION		2	
PATHWAYS CERT. COMP.: NETWORK MANAGEMENT		2	
PATHWAYS CERT. COMP.: SOFTWARE SUPPORT		1	
PATHWAYS CERT. COMP.: TECHNICAL SUPPORT		3	
PATHWAYS CERT. COMP.: WEBSITE FUNDAMENTALS		1	
PATHWAYS CERT. COMP.: SUPERVISION		1	

SOUTHWESTERN
Oregon Community College

Directory

1. Stensland Hall
2. Dellwood Hall
3. Randolph Hall
4. Empire Hall / Lakeview Rooms / Hales Center for the Performing Arts
5. Tioga Hall
6. Sitkum Hall
7. Coaledo Hall
8. Eden Hall
9. Lampa Hall
10. B-2 Electronics Tech Lab
11. Greenhouse
12. Sunset Hall
13. Sumner Hall
14. Fairview Hall
15. Tennis Courts
16. Field House
17. Fire Science
18. Baseball Field
19. Fire Tower
20. Softball Field
21. Prosper Hall / Gym
22. Poet's Eye Outdoor Theater
23. B-3 Maintenance Warehouse
24. Umpqua Hall
25. Student Recreation Center
26. Track / Soccer Field
27. Plant Services / Maintenance
28. Greenhouse
29. Newmark Center
30. Family Center / Child Care
31. Oregon Coast Culinary Institute

STUDENT HOUSING:

32. North Head
33. Lighthouse Depot
34. Willamette River
35. Warrior Rock
36. Desdemona Sands
37. Point Adams
38. Tillamook Rock
39. Cape Meares
40. Yaquina Head
41. Heceta Head
42. Umpqua River
43. Cape Arago
44. Coquille River
45. Cape Blanco
46. St. George Reef
47. Battery Point
48. Trinidad Head
49. Willapa Bay
50. Gray's Harbor

51. Neighborhood Facility Building

* Denotes Disabled Accessible Entrances
≡ Denotes Stairs

EMPIRE LAKE

N COLLEGE WAY
S COLLEGE WAY
W COLLEGE WAY
STUDENT WAY
E COLLEGE WAY
E ENTRY WAY
M ENTRY WAY

NEWMARK AVENUE

PUBLIC PARKING LOT #1
PUBLIC PARKING LOT #2
PUBLIC PARKING LOT #3
PUBLIC PARKING LOT #4

BUS STOP

← WEST
EAST →

185

Reference List:

(1) Community Colleges - The History of Community Colleges, The junior college and the research university. The Community College Mission http://education.stateuniversity.com/pages/1873/Community-Colleges.html

(2) http://www.oah.org/pubs/commcoll/mock.html

(3) Hakanson, Dr. John W. Oregon's Community College: Their Beginnings and Growth, 1986.

(4) The Coquille Valley Sentinel, January 1, 1966.

(5) The World Newspaper, January 22, 1966 , "Highlights of SWOCC's History" by Sydney D. Thompson.

(6) The World Newspaper, May 3, 1967, "Brookins Raps Coquille Vote" by Phyllis Countryman.

(7) The World Newspaper, February 2, 1963.

(8) North Bend News, June 15, 1967, "Journeymen Carpenters start MDTA 20-week course session at SWOCC".

(9) The World Newspaper, February 22, 1963.

(10) The Empire Builder, September 14, 1967.

(11) Accreditation Committee of the "Higher Commission, Northwest Association of Secondary and Higher Schools" report, 1966.

(12) The Courier, February 9, 1967.

(13) The Southwester, April 23, 1981.

(14) Lansing, William A., "Seeing the Forest for the Trees", Monroe Press, Eugene, Oregon, 2005.

(15) Living History tapes on file at Southwestern Oregon Community College.

(16) http://library.thinkquest.org/22522/

(17) http://kclibrary.lonestar.edu/decade80.html

(18) The World Newspaper, July 14, 1961, "SWOCC Budget is Approved".

(19) http://lanecc.edu/archives/OH-ParnellD.html

(20) Long Range Plan for Development of South Western Oregon College, 1961.

(21) State Board of Education ruling establishing the Southwestern Oregon Education District, August 5, 1960.

(22) A progress report from Southwestern Oregon Community College prepared for the Commission on Higher Schools Northwest Association of Secondary and Higher Schools, May 31, 1968.

(23) Living History Tape of Jeff Manley, interviewed April 12, 1984.

(24) Robbins, William G., "Hard Times in Paradise", University of Washington Press, Seattle, Washington, 1998.

(25) http://bluebook.state.or.us/cultural/history/history28.htm

(26) http://www.aia.org/aiaucmp/groups/aia/documents/pdf/aiab082110.pdf

(27) http://www.1970sflashback.com/1972/Potpourri.asp

(28) http://www.oregon.gov/CCWD/pdf/Viewbook/CommunityCollegeViewbook2009-10.pdf

(29) The Oregon Community College Association 503-399-9912

(30) http://www.qualityinfo.org/olmisj/ArticleReader?itemid=00006417

(31) http://cougartown.com/slang.html

(32) http://www.inthe70s.com/generated/terms.shtml

(33) http://www.inthe80s.com/glossary.shtml

(34) http://www.inthe90s.com/generated/terms.shtml

(35) http://people.howstuffworks.com/53-slang-terms-by-decade.htm

(36) SWOCC student handbook, 1965.

(37) Spindrift, 1970-71.

(38) The Southwester, a souvenir edition, 1965.

(39) The World Newspaper, January 22, 1966, "A Pictorial Salute to Progress – Southwestern Oregon Community College".

(40) The World Newspaper, Horizon, May 1981.

(41) http://www.league.org/league/projects/ccti/projects/files/SOCC_Case_Study.pdf

(42) The World Newspaper, May 1, 1981, Horizon Special Insert.

(42) Preus, Camille 2007. Two Oregon Governors: The Role of Perceptions in Community College State Budget Development. Doctor of Education Dissertation. Department of Education Oregon State University.

(43) Transcribed interview with Helen W. Ferguson, September 23, 1978, on file at SWOCC.

(44) The World Newspaper, March 26, 1960, by Linda Meierjurgen.

(45) The World Newspaper, February 3, 1990, by Greg Gerson.

(46) The World Newspaper, September 25, 1991, by Nancy Kemper.

(47) The Southwester, June 7, 1991, Portable Math Kits.

(48) The World Newspaper, September 25, 1991, by John Gunther.

(49) Register Guard Newspaper, August 30, 1990, by Lance Robertson.

(50) The Southwester, November 7, 1985.

(51) Southwestern Oregon Community College News and 1991 Fall Class Schedule.

(52) Southwestern Oregon Community College News ca. 1978 interview with Bob Croft.

(53) Nathan Douthit 6/11/2010 personal correspondence.

(54) The Courier, December 5, 1978.

(55) The World Newspaper, September 20, 1971 page 5.

(56) The Curry Coastal Pilot, July 20, 1996.

(57) Interview of Jesse Laird by Patrick Coble, December 1978, "History of the College".

(58) Interview of Robert Croft by Patrick Coble, September 18, 1978, "History of the College".

(59) Interview of Roger Spaugh by Patrick Coble, October 5, 1978, "History of the College".

(60) Interview of Ron Lilienthal by Patrick Coble, October 12, 1978, "History of the College".

(61) Interview of Bernell Meacham by Patrick Coble, October 3, 1978, "History of the College".

(62) Interview of Ralph Stuller by Patrick Coble, December 7, 1978, "History of the College".

(63) Interview of Bill Jordon by Patrick Coble, January 25, 1979, "History of the College".

(64) Interview of Don Moffitt by Patrick Coble, October 18, 1978, "History of the College".

(65) The World Newspaper, South Coast Week, March 9, 1983.

(66) Vocational-Technical and Related General Education in Southwestern Oregon College by Oregon Department of Education, May 1962.

(67) Myrtle Point Herald Newspaper, January 19, 1986, "Powers High Starts Telecommunications Project".

(68) The World Newspaper, July 31, 1986, "Year of Transition at College".

(69) The North Bend News, April 15, 1981, "North Bend Firefighters to Train at SWOCC Fire Tower".

(70) The World Newspaper, February 2, 2001, "College Wants Taste of Culinary Arts Business".

(71) The Herald Newspaper, March 26, 1981, "Economic Climate Hurts Local College".

(72) The World Newspaper, July 25, 1992, Public Forum, "Really Care About Students" by Clara Radcliffe PhD.

(73) The World Newspaper, April 11, 2000, "Newmark Center Receives Award".

(74) The World Newspaper, December 21, 1985, "Students Can Learn Via TV".

(75) The North Bend News, December 4, 1985, "Barber Installed SWOCC President".

(76) The World Newspaper, October 4, 2001, "Center Offers Businesses One-Stop Assistance".

(77) The World Newspaper, September 12 1981, "SWOCC Celebrates the Progress of 20 Years".

(78) The World Newspaper, August 14, 2010 "OCCI Team Will Represent USA at Culinary Olympics".

(79) The World Newspaper, June 10, 1978, "Indian Workshop Due in Bay Area".

(80) The World Newspaper, March 16, 1991, "Coos Bay Skills Center Helps Unemployed".

(81) The Curry County Pilot, November 1, 1997, "Southwestern Oregon Community College".

(82) The World Newspaper, March 14, 1975 page 15a.

(83) http://www.globalsecurity.org/military/facility/north-bend.htm

(84) The World Newspaper, December 21, 1974 page 1, photo courtesy of the Coos Historical and Maritime Museum.

(85) Scott, Patricia M., 2003. Perceptions and Experiences of Students Who Graduate with the Associate of Arts/ Oregon Transfer (AA/OT) Degree. Oregon State University in partial fulfillment of the requirements for the degree of Doctor of Education. UMI, ProQuest Information and Learning Company, Ann Arbor, MI. 48106

INDEX

A

B

C

Computer Science (CS) 132, 154, 175

Coos Art Museum 160

Crim, Harvey x, 30, 46

Croft, Robert 9, 18-19, 22, 24, 38, 88, 92, 176, 183

CS (Computer Science) 132, 154, 175

Curry County 5, 89, 102, 116, 125, 149-58

Curry County Campus xvi, 2, 29, 89, 99, 113-15, 146, 149-50, 152-8

D

Dellwood Hall 35, 37, 40, 53-6, 60

Distance learning 80, 82, 104, 115

Distinguished Alumnus 146-8

Douthit, Nathan 70-1, 81, 183

E

Earth Day 73, 75

EBB Tide 24

Eden Hall 93-5

Empire 8, 17, 29-30, 40, 49, 57, 82

Empire Hall 58, 90-1, 93-4, 141

Empire Lakes xvi, 17-19, 24, 29-31, 33, 36, 40, 52, 58, 60, 64, 68, 76-8, 90-1, 97

Expressions West 160-1

F

Faculty Senate 24-5, 41, 65, 174

Family Center 130-3

Ferguson, Helen 18, 40-1, 66, 77, 92, 107, 176, 182

Fire Tower 95

Fishing industries 52, 70, 86, 89, 91, 96-7, 99-100, 145

Florence 3, 5, 7-8, 129

Floyd, Melvin 4-5

Forest products industry 30, 37, 49, 51-2, 75-6, 85, 89, 113, 122

Forest technology program 28, 51, 73, 75-8, 95, 107, 116

Foundation vii, 21, 42, 100, 121, 140, 142, 159-60, 163, 168

FTE (Full Time Equivalent) xiv, 17, 73, 100, 105-6, 115-19, 125, 127-9, 143, 150, 152-4, 164-5

[Created with TExtract / www.Texyz.com]